Patti Gallagher Mansfield

PROCLAIM the Joy of the Gospel!

Spirit-Filled Evangelizers

Proclaim the Joy of the Gospel!
Spirit-Filled Evangelizers
Patti Gallagher Mansfield

Copyright © 1987, 2004, 2014, Patti Gallagher Mansfield. All rights reserved.

Cover image: Shutterstock.com
Cover and book design: Amor Deus Publishing Design Department

No part of this book may be reproduced, stored in a retrieval system or transmitted in any form or by any means - electronic, mechanical, photocopying, recording, or otherwise - without written permission of the publisher.

For information regarding permission, write to:
Amor Deus Publishing
Attention: Permissions Dept.
4727 North 12th Street
Phoenix, AZ 85014

ISBN 978-1-61956-248-6

Second Edition August 2014
10 9 8 7 6 5 4 3 2

Original edition entitle *Proclaim His Marvelous Deeds*, published by Franciscan University Press, Stubenville, Ohio © 1987.

Published and printed in the United States of America by Amor Deus Publishing an imprint of Vesuvius Press Incorporated.

♻ Text printed on 30% post-consumer waste recycled paper.

For additional inspirational books visit us at AmorDeus.com

Dedication

*To Father Jim Ferry,
of happy memory, who always encouraged me
to share my personal testimony.*

Endorsements

The dictionary defines witness as "to give or afford evidence of." By virtue of our Baptism we are all called to be witnesses *who give evidence of the joy, hope, and power of the Gospel message. But how? And that is the question Patti Gallagher Mansfield answers for us in this treasure of a primer on evangelization. Instructional, practical, and succinct, through its pages readers discover the "whys" of personal evangelization as well as the essentials of developing and delivering an inspiring personal testimony of their own. Always the evangelizer herself, Patti gives more as well. Tucked into her explanations as well as through the poignant examples of testimony she offers, Patti "fans into flame" the faith of her readers and encourages them to be men and women "for such a time as this," proclaimers of the joy of the Gospel!*

Johnnette S. Benkovic
Founder, Women of Grace®
Host, EWTN Television and Radio

More timely than ever. It is urgent that every Catholic learn to "tell their story" in a way that elicits faith in others. Patti Mansfield has been "telling her story" for many years now with great effect and can help all of us do so more effectively. A must read for the New Evangelization!

Ralph Martin, STD
President, Renewal Ministries

Patti Mansfield practices what she teaches and does both in a superb manner. She is the witness, par excellence, of God's action in the Catholic Charismatic Renewal. She has been a student and teacher of witnessing for decades. Everyone can learn from reading this book and everyone can use what he or she learns. This is a respectful, inspiring and useful work. Read on!

Fr. Michael Scanlan, TOR
Chancellor Emeritus
Franciscan University of Steubenville

Introduction

"The Pope is talking about Mom!" my daughter exclaimed to my husband as they sat in Rome's Olympic Stadium in the midst 52,000 people at an international conference of the Catholic Charismatic Renewal on June 1, 2014. She had a headset for translation from Italian into English which was working. My husband and I had headsets that did not work. At that moment we were not seated together because I was a speaker at the event, and those taking part in the program were placed in the front row in order to greet the Pope.

As Pope Francis began his address in Italian I thought I heard my name, but I could scarcely believe my ears. I turned to the Argentinian woman next to me who understood Italian and asked her, "Did the Pope just mention my name?" She excitedly confirmed, "Yes!" Not until I returned home a week later did I see the full translation of his text in which he said, "I am grateful also for the presence of the first who had an intense experience of the power of the Holy Spirit; I believe that it was Patti who is here…"

Quite beyond the personal joy of hearing my name on the lips of Pope Francis, was the joy of discovering that he knows the Charismatic Renewal "from the inside." He knows our history (the Renewal began at a retreat in 1967 at which I was present). He knows our mission (to bring the grace of a Personal Pentecost to the whole Church.)

He told us he felt "at home" as he joined us in singing his favorite Charismatic Renewal song in Spanish, *"Vive Jesús el Señor"* with his hands lifted in a charismatic gesture of prayer. And, so characteristic of this humble man, he knelt while the assembly prayed for a new outpouring of the Holy Spirit upon him, in song, in Italian, and then in the gift of tongues. It was a truly moving and inspiring experience!

In the Pope's address, he affirmed the Renewal in unequivocal terms, "You were born of the will of the Spirit as 'a current of grace' in the Church and for the Church." Then the Holy Father told us what he expects of us. Following are his exact words:

> **The first thing is conversion to the love of Jesus, which changes life and makes of the Christian a witness of the Love of God.**
>
> **I expect from you that you share with all, in the Church, the grace of Baptism in the Holy Spirit (expression that is read in the Acts of the Apostles).**
>
> **I expect from you an evangelization with the Word of God which proclaims that Jesus is alive and loves all men.**

Hearing this I was emboldened to give him my letter (which you will see under my arm in the photo on the back cover). When he stood in front of me and took my hand I said, "I'm Patti" and he replied, "Oh, one of the first," and he pulled me to his chest to embrace me. Then I said, "Holy Father," and he leaned closer to hear me. "I have an idea to bring this grace of Baptism in the Spirit to the whole Church". I'm not sure he understood my English and he replied to me in Italian, which I didn't understand. But I handed my letter to the Archbishop behind him who handed it to a security guard. Perhaps Pope Francis will read it one day.

In the letter I explain that the grace of Baptism in the Spirit was released in the lives of millions of Catholics when David Mangan, a young graduate of Duquesne University on retreat with me in 1967, suggested that we "renew our sacrament of Confirmation." I am asking Pope Francis to call the whole Church, every Pentecost, to "renew our sacrament of Confirmation," in much the same way we renew our baptismal promises every Easter.

Whether or not that ever happens on the Feast of Pentecost in the universal Church, today each of us can renew our commitment to Jesus as our personal Lord and Savior and ask to be baptized in the Holy Spirit. This book, *Proclaim the Joy of the Gospel!* is a response to the Pope's mandate to share with the whole Church the grace of the Baptism in the Spirit. We need a New Pentecost for a New Evangelization!

Here you will read the stories of people from all walks of life and all ages who have met the living Lord Jesus and who have been filled with His Spirit. You will learn how to give your personal testimony like they have and become part of a vast throng of "Spirit-filled evangelizers"! Get ready for a wonderful adventure as you welcome the Holy Spirit more deeply into your life and begin to witness to His love.

Patti Gallagher Mansfield
August 15, 2014
Feast of the Assumption

Proclaim The Joy Of The Gospel!

The Church exists to evangelize! *You* exist to evangelize too! I am more convinced than ever that your personal testimony is the single most important tool you have in evangelization. In this book you will learn how to share the joy of the Gospel with others by giving your testimony! About now you may be saying, "Not me! I have no testimony!" But if you are a Christian, if you are a Catholic, let me assure you that you *do* have a testimony. You have a story to tell about what Jesus has done in your life.

There's a marvelous old hymn entitled, "I Love to Tell the Story." I pray that as you read the testimonies in this book and prepare your own testimony, you will get excited about looking for opportunities to "tell the story." We are living in a time in which every man, woman and child is called to be a witness to the risen Savior, Jesus Christ. Every pope in recent decades has stressed the importance of the New Evangelization. Just listen!

Blessed Pope Paul VI stated in *On Evangelization in the Modern World, 41*:

> "**Modern man listens more willingly to witnesses than to teachers, and if he does listen to teachers, it is because they are witnesses."**
>
> **Pope Saint John Paul II has said, "If you have met Jesus Christ, proclaim Him to the world!"**

Pope Benedict XVI explains, "To the extent that we nourish ourselves on Christ and are in love with him, we feel within us the incentive to bring others to him: Indeed, we cannot keep the joy of the faith to ourselves; we must pass it on."

Pope Francis wrote his Apostolic Exhortation, *The Joy of the Gospel*, 259, that he wanted to mobilize the whole Church to be "Spirit-filled evangelizers…evangelizers fearlessly open to the working of the Holy Spirit."

Perhaps you've heard this statement before. It's shocking but true. You are the only Bible some people will ever read. It is the manner in which the gospel message has taken flesh in you, that will convince certain people that Jesus is alive. As a full-time evangelizer, I spend much of my time speaking at conferences and this usually involves getting up on a stage. While you may not be called to speak to thousands of people at one time, I can assure you of this: You will be called a thousand times to bear witness. Your stage may be in line at the grocery store, in a doctor's office, at the gas station or in your kitchen. In the years remaining to each of us, God will give us a thousand opportunities to tell others that Jesus is alive and that His love and mercy are there for everyone.

In *Novo Millenio Ineunte*, Pope Saint John Paul II, has presented us with a wonderful vision for the new millennium. He's calling on each member of the Body of Christ to get serious about holiness and about evangelization. His watchword for this new millennium has been: "Put out into the deep and lower your nets for a catch!" (Luke 5:4). How can you put out into the deep? Through prayer! How can you lower your nets for a catch? Through evangelism! If you've picked up this book it means you want to learn how to evangelize. Now, be prepared to lower your nets by learning how to give your personal testimony.

May the of the testimonies in this book inspire you to remember the mercies of the Lord toward you and to proclaim the joy of the Gospel in word and deed.

A New Pentecost for a New Evangelization

"My soul magnifies the Lord, and my spirit rejoices in God my Savior, for He has regarded the low estate of His handmaiden. For behold, henceforth all generations will call me blessed; for He who mighty has done great things for me, and holy is His name" (Luke 1:46-49).

This is the beginning of the "testimony" of Mary, the Mother of Jesus as recorded for us in the first chapter of St. Luke. After having conceived Jesus by the power of the Holy Spirit, we are told that "Mary arose and went with haste into the hill country" (Luke 1:39). Where was she off to in such a hurry? Mary was going to give her testimony for the first time to Elizabeth, her kinswoman. She was impelled by the Spirit of God to witness to Elizabeth about the marvels God had done in her and to confirm God's action in Elizabeth.

And so it is throughout the history of God's dealings with His people. When a person has been deeply touched by the Living God the immediate response is to go "with haste" to tell someone about the good news of God's mercy. The people of God have been giving testimony for generations, and so the faith has spread.

I knew as I was growing up that giving witness was part of my calling as a Christian. But in my own Catholic experience "giving witness" translated into explaining to my Protestant friends why I couldn't eat meat on Friday. Or it might have meant having the courage to make the Sign of the Cross before meals while at table with a Jewish classmate. I didn't realize that giving witness had to focus in on the heart of the matter—namely, my relationship with the Lord Jesus Christ. Nor did I realize that it was not enough to give witness to Christ by one's way of life alone, but that the Catholic laity are called to look for opportunities to announce Christ through the spoken word as well (Second Vatican Council, *Document on the Laity, 13*).

Blessed Pope Paul VI made this very clear when he wrote:

> **The Good News proclaimed by the witness of life sooner or later has to be proclaimed by the Word of life. There is no true evangelization if the name, the teaching, the life, the promises, the kingdom and the mystery of Jesus of Nazareth, the Son of God are not proclaimed.**
> (*On Evangelization in the Modern World, 22*)

What convinced me that I had to be a witness for Christ was my experience of a "Personal Pentecost." It was my happy privilege to be present on a student retreat during my junior year at Duquesne University in Pittsburgh, Pennsylvania. We were studying the Acts of the Apostles and began to question why we didn't experience the power of the Holy Spirit like the early Christians did. As I knelt in the retreat house chapel on February 18, 1967, and surrendered myself unconditionally to Jesus Christ, He baptized me in His Holy Spirit. I arose to my feet a new person and from that moment on, my life has never been the same. My "New Pentecost" led to a "New Evangelization." It always does. The Holy Spirit pushes us out into mission! And I'm not the only one to have had this experience!

That student retreat has become known around the world as the "Duquesne Weekend" and it marked the beginning of the Catholic Charismatic Renewal. Since 1967 over 120 million Catholics in 235 countries around the world have experienced this tremendous grace of being baptized in the Holy Spirit. Through the new outpouring of the Holy Spirit, God is raising up a people who are able to proclaim His marvelous deeds to all the nations.

The Charismatic Renewal is the largest of the ecclesial movements which have come into being since Vatican II. There are now millions of Catholics, baptized in the Spirit, who want to get to "the heart of the matter". Our deepest desire is to share with others what God, in His mercy, has done for us. We are convinced that the graces we have experienced in the Baptism in the Holy Spirit are meant for every man, woman and child on the face of the earth today! And apparently, Pope Francis is also convinced that what he calls "the current of grace" in the Catholic Charismatic Renewal is for everyone. That "current of grace" is the Person of the Holy Spirit and the Spirit belongs to the whole Church!!

In April 1967, just a few weeks after I was baptized in the Holy Spirit, I was visiting for the holidays with my family in New Jersey. Ralph Martin, a Catholic layman involved in evangelism, was also in New Jersey. I had met Ralph just a few weeks earlier when he came to Duquesne University and we shared with him about the Baptism in the Holy

Proclaim The Joy Of The Gospel!

Spirit. Ralph brought me to a small prayer meeting at Fordham University in New York City. To my knowledge, the participants had not yet experienced the outpouring of the Holy Spirit as we had on the Duquesne Weekend.

As we mounted the steps to the meeting Ralph said to me, "Patti, I want you to share your testimony tonight." I drew a complete blank. "What's my testimony?" I replied. Ralph then explained to me as we approached the door of the meeting, "Just tell them what happened to you in the chapel at the retreat at Duquesne. Tell them how God touched you." And so that night at a prayer meeting at Fordham University, I learned from Ralph what it meant to "give testimony," and I've been giving it ever since.

Unlike our Protestant and Pentecostal friends, we Catholics have not been trained in *how* to give a testimony. It's not part of our Eucharistic worship or catechetical instruction. As we've entered into the Charismatic Renewal we have had to learn what it means to give a personal testimony and how to do it effectively. Knowing how to present the story of what the Lord means in your life is not only important in the context of a prayer meeting or special event, it's an essential tool in witnessing about Jesus to people in your everyday life. You and I are called to proclaim the joy of the Gospel to others on a daily basis so that they may come to have faith in the Lord.

The following guidelines on how to give a personal testimony are gleaned from my own experience of sharing my story many hundreds of times for almost 50 years. These principles apply to speaking at a public gathering as well as in person-to-person evangelism. Your first job is to learn how to give your testimony. Then you can be ready to give it in a short form on a moment's notice.

Your Attitude

"Your attitude must be that of Christ," St. Paul tells us (Philipians 2:5). Jesus came as a servant, humbly laying down his life for His friends. He had no concern for His own glory. His concern was for His Father and for us, His friends. As you are preparing to give your testimony, take on the attitude of our Lord Jesus Christ and say, "Lord, not because I am worthy, but because of Your great mercy, I will speak to my brothers and sisters about You." Look upon any opportunity of bearing witness as a way to serve God's people. What you are to do is not to exalt and glorify yourself but rather to exalt and glorify the Lord Jesus Christ.

I once heard a man give his personal testimony and the focus was more on himself than on the Lord. The poor fellow had the unenviable task of following an excellent speaker. To compensate he began by saying, "Step aside, brother, and make room for me!" He then proceeded to take twice the length of time allotted to give his testimony accompanied by plenty of dramatics. At one point he asked the people, "You don't want to go home tonight, do you?" Without waiting for their reply, he continued at great length. It turned out many of his listeners *did* want to go home. This is a man in whom the Lord has done a great work, and God continues to use him. However, on this particular occasion, his preoccupation with being as popular as another speaker led him to put too much of the focus on himself. This was probably due to inexperience more than anything else.

I try to repeat these words from Psalm 115 while preparing to speak, "Not to us, O Lord, not to us but to Your Name give glory." The focus should not be on yourself, neither your accomplishments, nor your unworthiness, but simply on what God in His mercy has done for you. In giving testimony at a public meeting, the tendency in most people is to spend a great deal of time explaining how nervous or unworthy they feel. This takes up valuable time. Without meaning to, people who do this only succeed in drawing attention to themselves.

If you've been asked to give your testimony at a gathering, be confident that people want to hear you. They understand your nervousness already. You *are* unworthy; but then so is everyone else! We are all still in the process of growing in holiness. It is impossible to wait until all our problems are solved before giving a testimony. That day will not come. After having humbled yourself before God, present yourself to your brothers and sisters simply as a fellow servant ready to lay down your life for them by rendering this service. "For what we preach is not ourselves but Jesus Christ as Lord, with ourselves as your servants for Jesus' sake" (II Corinthians 4:5).

Sometimes people are afraid that if they tell about the great things God has done for them or about the way the Lord has used them, it may seem like they are bragging. This false sense of humility keeps them back from sharing their personal testimony. If you tell your story in the right way you will *not* be saying, "Look at me!" but rather "Look at Jesus! Admire Him! Be in awe of Him! What He's done for me, He will do for you!" As Scripture says, "Let him who would boast, boast in the Lord" (I Corinthians 1:31).

Two of my close friends, Abner and Kathleen Fandal, served as Catholic Chaplains in a hospital. Whenever they shared a testimony about their ministry to the sick, I was moved to greater faith in the Lord. Even though they happened to be the instruments that God was using, the focus was never on themselves, but always on the Lord. For example, they gave the following testimony: "We met a young woman in the hospital who had serious burns. We placed the Blessed Sacrament on her burns and prayed. Then we gave her Holy Communion. Her skin was healed significantly by the next day and she was released much sooner than expected; praise God!" Now, that's a testimony that glorifies God!

The attitudes we need to have in giving a personal testimony are those of humility, service and confidence. Of course, these are attitudes we need to develop for every aspect of our Christian lives. The occasion of giving testimony can be a time of deep spiritual growth as we yield to the action of the Holy Spirit. Recalling what the Lord has done for us can help make us more humble, grateful and willing to serve Him. Many people think their own story is not especially noteworthy. But once they begin to reflect on all the Lord has done for them, they realize His tremendous goodness. Giving a personal testimony can help make us more aware of God's presence in our lives and build our faith.

Prepare Prayerfully

Pope Francis writes in *The Joy of the Gospel*, 262, "Spirit-filled evangelizers are evangelizers who pray and work." Prayer is an essential part of preparing to give a personal testimony or to render any service to the Lord. It is in prayer that God can help you develop the right attitudes. It is in prayer that He can remind you of certain events from your life that He would want you to share. It is in prayer that He will bring to mind special Scripture passages for you to use on this occasion. I believe that the more I seek the Lord in prayer, the more powerfully God can use me no matter what words I may speak.

As you pray, seek God for three specific things:

First, seek God for His presence and His anointing upon you.

Some of the most moving personal testimonies I have ever heard were not given by people with great oratorical skills. However, the anointing of God was upon them with such power that I knew I was listening to the Lord's special servants. God touched me *through* them because His presence was so much *with* them.

Shortly after I was baptized in the Holy Spirit two men visited our prayer group. They had been in the Spirit many years and knew the Lord in an intimate way. These were simple men. They were not well-educated or well-dressed. From their hearts they spoke about having a relationship of love and obedience with Jesus Christ. I was deeply affected by their testimony.

A few days later a well-known author came to campus to speak about Christianity. The student union was packed with people eager to hear what he had to say. For about an hour this gentleman, of considerable fame and prestige, theorized about Jesus and His gospel. The presentation lacked power and life. It was empty. If this speaker had a relationship with the Lord, it was not reflected in what he said that night. However smooth and articulate he might have been, he could not draw others to Jesus Christ as effectively as our two simple visitors to the prayer meeting.

St. Paul tells us how he came to the Corinthians in "great fear and trembling" not relying on any power of his own to speak or to convince but only with "a demonstration of the power of the Spirit" (I Corinthians 2:1-5). God's presence and His anointing made the difference. In Acts 4, when Peter and John were brought before the Sanhedrin after healing the cripple, they spoke with conviction proclaiming the name of Jesus. The Scripture tells us, "Observing the self-assurance of Peter and John, and realizing that the speakers were uneducated men of no standing, the questioners were amazed. Then they recognized these men as having been with Jesus" (Acts 4:13). Being with Jesus and receiving the anointing of the Holy Spirit gave Peter and John the power to bear witness with assurance, even before their enemies.

We can be with this same Jesus today in prayer! We can ask with confidence for the power of His Holy Spirit to be upon us as we speak. Though we may be "of no standing" like Peter and John, people will recognize us as having been with Jesus. Your first priority then is to seek God for His presence and His anointing upon you. My spiritual director likes to remind me when I become fearful of giving testimony, especially to priests and bishops, "The anointing is everything!"

Second, seek God for His blessing on all those who will hear you.

A few years ago I was asked to give my testimony at a brunch for Catholic women. In the weeks preceding this event I found that I was spending a good bit of time thinking about what I would wear and how I would fix my hair for the day of the brunch. I had to make an effort to focus my attention on the Lord. Every time I would begin to think about my hair, I would turn myself back to the Lord and ask Him to bless the women, my sisters in Christ, who would be at the brunch that day. Ask the Lord to give you a share of His own love for the people who will hear you.

Each time I give my testimony I pray that those listening will actually *experience for themselves* the grace that I received when God poured out His Holy Spirit upon us at Duquesne. I pray, "Lord, let this be more than a nice story about an event that happened long ago. Even as I speak about how Your love touched me *then*, may Your love touch them *now*." It's important to do more than recount events of the past. Desire to draw your listeners into a closer relationship with the Lord. That loving concern to bring them to Jesus will be communicated as you speak.

I also have begun to invoke the assistance of the angels each time I speak about the Lord. I call on the Archangels: St. Michael, St. Gabriel and St. Raphael. I call on my own angels and the guardian angels of all who will be attending. St. Francis de Sales recommended this as a helpful practice and it is!

I also place myself in the Immaculate Heart of Mary. I ask her to purify my own words with her purity so that what passes through me might reach the hearts of my listeners most effectively. As a Mother, she will do this for us.

Third, seek God for His guidance as to what to say and what not to say at this particular time to this particular group.

I don't believe I have ever given my testimony the same way twice. In fact, I'm often surprised at the particular things God leads me to emphasize on certain occasions. Afterwards, the Lord usually confirms through someone who was listening that the specific Scripture passage or event I shared ministered to a personal need.

If you don't know the group you are going to address, ask the leader to tell you something about the ages and backgrounds of the participants. Use good common sense in suiting your remarks to the group you are addressing. For example, when speaking to young people, I'd probably begin with something from my experience as a student. When speaking to women, I would use an example from my life as a wife and mother. In an ecumenical setting, I'd be careful to emphasize points that could be accepted by Christians of all denominations.

However, beyond what our own sensitivity and understanding prompts us to share, the Holy Spirit wants to inspire us. In *The Joy of the Gospel 280*, Pope Francis wrote, "The Holy Spirit knows well what is needed in every time and place. This is what it means to be mysteriously fruitful!"

Seek the Lord for wisdom about what would be most helpful to your listeners at this time and you will receive the guidance you need. St. James tells us, "If any of you is without wisdom, let him ask God who gives generously and ungrudgingly to all, and it will be given him" (James 1:5).

Organize Your Thoughts

It's true that the Holy Spirit can directly inspire you as to what to say while you are on your feet speaking. I have experienced it. Sometimes you don't know beforehand that you will be called upon to give testimony. In this case you simply trust that the Lord will show you what to say as you open your mouth. In witnessing to people in your everyday life you rarely have time to prepare your words. However, if you are asked in advance to give a personal testimony at a meeting, this is a different set of circumstances. After prayer, you should take pen in hand and organize your thoughts.

I am *not* necessarily suggesting that you write your testimony word for word and then read it. This can make for a very boring presentation. But I *am* suggesting that you organize your thoughts on paper in the form of notes. I have found this extremely helpful.

One way to begin is simply to write down scattered thoughts, passages and incidents that have been coming to you either in prayer or as you go about your daily work. These scattered thoughts can serve as raw material for your testimony. Unfortunately, many a testimony never gets beyond this stage and what is presented sounds like scattered thoughts with no cohesion.

Your next step is to sort through and organize these thoughts into some logical order. Usually a chronology is helpful—before, during, and after meeting the Lord in a more personal way. However, in some people's lives the growth came so gradually that a chronology tends to be boring, and another mode of organizing thoughts is more effective.

You may try to present your testimony in the form of some significant lessons you have learned from the Lord in your life. A helpful tool in putting together your testimony is to consider if there are a few key Scripture passages which have changed your life. You might build your presentation around these particular passages. A few well-chosen Scripture passages can be very powerful in bringing people face–to–face with the Lord. Ask the Holy Spirit to guide you. "The Word of God is living and active!" (Hebrews 4:12). A good testimony should include some quotes from the Scripture.

Another way to present your testimony is to highlight several areas which have changed since you have surrendered more fully to Jesus and the power of His Spirit. For instance, I remember hosting a speaker at the high school where I was teaching years ago. After one class my students told me they couldn't hear her because she was so soft-spoken. She laughed and related this change: "Before I knew Jesus personally and was baptized in the Spirit, I used to speak in a loud, brash tone that no one could bear. Now that I've met Him, I need a microphone to be heard! He has made me gentle!" What a beautiful transformation!

My own notes usually consist of several main points and Scripture passages that are marked with a highlighter pen so that, at a glance, I can refer to them while speaking. I recently heard a powerful testimony that was written out word for word on note cards. The speaker was so well-prepared that her talk was lively and dynamic even though she was following her notes very carefully. She maintained good eye contact with the people and probably managed to say more in the time allotted than she could have without her notes.

Watch Your Time

The shorter your allotted time to speak, the more important it is to discipline your thoughts and choose carefully what you will say. Be sure to respect the time limits imposed on you by those in leadership. It's not necessary to tell everything that has happened in your life in order to give a good personal testimony. And it is not quenching the Holy Spirit to obey a request from the leader to keep your testimony brief. Some friends who are prayer group leaders asked me to capitalize the last two sentences! It often happens that once a person begins to speak and gets some positive response from the audience, such as laughter, he or she will relax. Being relaxed while speaking is great, but be sure not to become so relaxed that you forget the time. You may never know how much your testimony, even a short testimony, may affect another person.

I was asked to give my personal testimony at the Ecumenical Charismatic Conference in Kansas City in 1977 before a crowd of 55,000 people. Capuchin Fr. Raniero Cantalamessa was present at that event as an "observer." He had read my short testimony in a magazine on the way to the conference and he was struck by a passage I used: "Blessed are the eyes that see what you see." After that conference he was baptized in the Spirit and soon called to be Preacher to the Papal Household, a position he has held since the pontificate of Pope Saint John Paul II. He has told me that my testimony played a role in helping him overcome his diffidence toward the Charismatic Renewal. Can you imagine?

At the conference only three minutes were allotted to me at a general session. Never before did I need to prepare myself with such discipline. A copy of that three minute version of my testimony is contained in this booklet to help you see how much can be said in a short time.

Several years later I had the privilege of giving my testimony on a video tape being prepared for the Holy Father, Pope Saint John Paul II. This time I had to condense it to ninety seconds. Of all the times I have ever given witness, none is more precious to me than those ninety seconds for the Holy Father! *Any* amount of time is long enough to give glory to the Lord if you prayerfully and carefully prepare.

Your testimony should consist of three parts: the beginning, the middle and the end. I know this may seem obvious, but the fact is, it is not! I've heard many a forty-five minute testimony in which the first forty minutes were spent in introduction. For example, one beautiful Spirit-filled woman, the mother of eleven children, was asked to give her testimony in forty-five minutes. Unfortunately, she got bogged down in details concerning the early part of her life. When forty minutes had passed she had only recounted the birth of three of her eleven children. With eight births to go plus the Baptism in the Holy Spirit, it was an eventful five minute conclusion! Needless to say, the middle and end of her testimony had to be crammed together. This could have been avoided if she had made better use of her time and planned a beginning, a middle, and an end.

It may be helpful to take your time frame and break it into three parts. For example, if I have fifteen minutes, I'll spend five minutes sharing my background and what life was like before I made a personal commitment to Christ. Then I'll spend five minutes sharing what happened when I allowed

Jesus free reign in me and was baptized in the Holy Spirit. In my last five minutes, I'll tell how my life was changed since then and encourage my listeners to believe that Jesus can change their lives too.

Of course, this particular breakdown of time is very arbitrary. You may well spend most of your time dealing with the events surrounding your deeper commitment to the Lord. Follow the lead of the Holy Spirit, not my plan.

The main point is simply this: within the time you have been allotted you will want to present a picture of where you were before your conversion, what happened at the time of conversion and what has changed since then.

Sometimes people take time to say a prayer from the microphone before they begin to speak. If the leader has already prayed for you, it's not necessary to do this. You may want to exhort people to give their lives to the Lord at the conclusion of your talk and say a brief prayer for them then. If you plan to use Scripture passages mark them beforehand to save time. It's always embarrassing to fumble through the pages of a Bible looking for a text while people are waiting.

I usually ask a friend within eye range to let me know by a nod if I am going too long. If you are at a podium, put out a watch or ask the moderator to help you keep track of time. Sometimes the leader can pass you a card when you have five minutes or one minute left. These are simply ways of respecting the order of the meeting you have been asked to address.

Keep It Simple

There is a real temptation to go into more detail than is necessary in a personal testimony. At times I've heard testimonies that were almost embarrassing because of the details that were shared. There are some things that are better saved for small, intimate gatherings of friends. Paint with broad strokes rather than a fine brush, especially about delicate matters. One of my friends who experienced a deep conversion and Baptism in the Spirit described his past life in this way. "I was seriously committed to a life of sin." This communicates a lot about his lifestyle without going into all the specifics.

A little dialogue goes a long way. Try to avoid excessive use of "Then he said, then I said, then he said." You don't have to tell what you were wearing and how the weather was unless it is important to your story.

Be simple. Be direct. Get to the heart of the matter: your relationship with the Lord Jesus Christ and the experience of the Baptism of the Holy Spirit. This is not a teaching. You are simply telling how God has acted in your life.

I want to say just a word about being natural in relating what happened to you. Don't be afraid to use some expression in your voice and face. I once heard a moving testimony of a woman whose husband left her. She persevered in prayer that the marriage would be restored. After several years, he repented, returned to her and they were remarried. Praise God! The only thing that detracted from this wonderful story was that she recounted everything in a monotone with no facial expression. When she finished I kept wondering if I heard her correctly. Did God really restore her marriage? If she could have let the joy and happiness which she obviously felt reflect in her tone of voice and countenance, it would have made her testimony more effective. So be natural. It's fine to smile about something great that Jesus did for you. People listen more readily to witnesses who look redeemed! Let your light shine!

In prayer one day I felt as if the Lord wanted to tell me something important about speaking on His behalf. I sensed that Jesus was saying something like this: "When you speak about me, speak with joy or do not speak at all." I try to remember this each time I have the chance to witness. No matter what trial I may be going through personally, when I speak about Jesus, I want "the Joy of the Gospel" to be communicated to His people. It is no wonder Pope Francis chose this title, *The Joy of the Gospel*, for his Apostolic Exhortation!

Terminology

As you think over God's action in your life be sure to acknowledge those ways the Lord was blessing you and providing for you before you made a personal commitment to Him. Sometimes we Catholics, in an effort to highlight the importance of what's happened to us in the Baptism in the Holy Spirit, make it sound as though we never experienced God's grace until the Charismatic Renewal.

If we were baptized and confirmed, if we participated in the Sacrament of Reconciliation and the Eucharist, then God's love and mercy were being poured into our lives, even if we didn't recognize it. The fact is that the Lord has been pursuing all of us in many ways long before we knew about the Baptism in the Spirit.

We can thank and praise God that through the Charismatic Renewal millions of Catholics have experienced deep conversion and a release of the Holy Spirit's power. But let us also thank and praise God that His grace has never left the Catholic Church over the ages. It's not necessary for you to go into a theological treatise about these things in your personal testimony. However, it is important for you to understand your experience in the context of God's grace which has been present to you in the Church long before you acknowledged it.

This means you should avoid saying things like: "I was baptized as an infant, but *I was just saved a year ago.*" "*I became a Christian* during the Life in the Spirit Seminar." "My life is wonderful these past two months since *I've been born again.*" Catholics who express their experience using this kind of terminology are easily misunderstood by other Catholics. What you are trying to communicate is that your personal decision to follow Jesus made a tremendous difference in your experience of Christian life.

Instead of using the terminology above you could say something like this: "Although I was baptized as an infant I didn't take my faith seriously until a year ago." "I started to experience the reality of what it means to be a Christian during the Life in the Spirit Seminar." "My life is wonderful these past two months since I've made an adult commitment to Jesus Christ." We want our words to be an avenue not an obstacle to help our friends and family come into a deeper life with God.

Be Discreet

It is very important to use great discretion and wisdom when sharing about past or present sin, your own or that of someone else. You do not want to give the devil glory or to ruin the reputation of another by exposing some sin or character defect. However, you do want to be honest about the struggles and difficulties you have faced. Insofar as is possible, speak of the Lord's dealings with you without revealing the weaknesses of those around you.

I recently heard a testimony by someone who has struggled with depression. This individual felt a significant relief after a healing service. Sharing this much would have been fine. However, this person went on to discuss the mental health issues of both spouse and in-laws. All this was done in innocence of course. I couldn't help but wonder if the spouse's employer were present or if the in-law's neighbors might be hearing this. Be prudent!

You may need to seek help from a pastoral leader as to how to share about particular situations in your life, for example, an alcoholic spouse or rebellious child. It's often helpful to go over your testimony with a friend who can lovingly assist you in bringing forth your story most effectively. "Let all you do be done in love," writes St. Paul (I Corinthians 16:14). The Lord will help you to be simple, direct, honest and loving to bring Him glory in what you say.

You're Ready

Now you are ready to give your testimony! You probably don't *feel* ready; we rarely do. Does it help you to know that even experienced public speakers get nervous before they give a talk? Take a deep breath. It's time to step out in faith. Instead of thinking of "all those people out there" try to imagine that you are speaking to just one person who really needs to know the Lord better. I once heard a wonderful bishop say that this thought helped him be more relaxed and natural in speaking to large groups.

I remember many years ago, my friend Father Jim Ferry, taught me the ABC's of speaking publicly.

- **A: *Audible.*** Don't be afraid to use the microphone. It won't bite! Most people stand too far away from a microphone. It should be directly in front of your mouth, close enough to lick if it were an ice cream cone! If the height of the microphone isn't right, ask the leader to adjust it for you.

- **B: *Brief.*** Watch your time. Going over by a few minutes isn't a problem. Talking twice the length of time allotted, however, is.

- **C: *Christ-centered.*** Lift up the person of Jesus Christ that others may come to know Him. Remember the words of Jesus in the Gospels, "Whoever acknowledges me before men I will acknowledge before my Father in heaven" (Matthew 10:32). What a privilege! Here is an opportunity to acknowledge Jesus publicly so that one day He will acknowledge you before the Father in heaven.

Here is just a final word about spiritual warfare. We Christians are in a battle as St. Paul tells us in Ephesians 6:10-20. Our fight is not against human forces but against the wiles of the devil. Often when someone is preparing to give a personal testimony he or she comes under attack by Satan. It may be a physical, emotional or spiritual harassment. Temptations and doubts may increase. Don't be surprised or upset by this. It is not uncommon. Know that in Jesus' Name you have authority over the power of the enemy. Plead the Blood of Jesus as protection and pray in the Name of Jesus for any work of the devil to be destroyed. "Thanks be to God who has given us the victory through our Lord Jesus Christ" (I Corinthians 15:57). You may go forth assured of that victory!

Look For Opportunities

You have learned how to tell your story. Now be ready to share it again and again. In I Peter 3:15-16 we are exhorted, "Should anyone ask you the reason for this hope of yours, *be ever ready to reply*, but speak gently and respectfully." Pray that the Lord will give you many opportunities to give witness to Him and then watch the Holy Spirit open doors before you!

My husband likes to say that the whole Gospel can be summed up in these two words: COME and GO. COME to Jesus, then GO to make disciples. I often pray in this way to respond to the call to COME and GO. When Jesus says, "Come", I reply, "Draw me!" When He says, "Go", I reply, "Use me." Try this prayer for yourself.

Look for those open doors, then walk through them. People need to know that God loves them and that Jesus died to save them from sin and death. Pope Saint John Paul II assures us of this need in every heart. "The missionary is convinced that, through the working of the Spirit, there already exists in individuals and peoples an expectation, even if an unconscious one, of knowing the truth about God, about man, and about how we are to be set free from sin and death" (*The Mission of the Redeemer*, 45).

In recent weeks I have had a chance to give my testimony to a man I met on an airplane. After some superficial conversation he began to ask me about my family and work. Finally he asked the leading question I had been waiting for, "What happened in your life to change you?" He posed this question about five minutes before landing!

In the few minutes remaining, I shared with him how Jesus had become the Lord of my life and what the Baptism in the Holy Spirit meant to me. He was very receptive to hearing about the Lord and as we parted there was a prayer in my heart for this man and his family.

Praise God for opportunities like these to touch just one life with the joy of the Gospel. I've often heard it said that the Lord is not looking for our *ability* so much as our *availability* to serve Him. Make yourself a servant who is available to hear the Master's call and to do His bidding.

Think about how you might tell your story in just one sentence so that you can be ready to give an explanation for the hope that is in you. A young woman came to me recently and told me her entire story in one sentence of introduction. "I am a pro-life Catholic who used to be an unchurched pro-abortion feminist!" Wow! Would that start a conversation! What is your one line testimony?

There is a new and powerful move of the Holy Spirit coming on the face of the earth. God wants all men and women to be saved and to come to the knowledge of the truth (cf. I Timothy 2:4). Countless people in the world have yet to hear the Good News of Jesus Christ. There are people in your family, your neighborhood and your office whom God wants to reach. You and I have been called "a chosen race, a royal priesthood, a holy nation, a people He claims for his own." And why have we been blessed? We have been blessed in order "to proclaim the glorious works of the One who called us from darkness into His marvelous light" (I Peter 2:9).

God has shown you His mercy so that you may become an instrument of His mercy to others who do not yet know, love and serve Him. Get prepared to be His witness! The Lord intends to use you and your personal testimony to touch many lives. He wants to equip you to proclaim the joy of the Gospel in the days and years ahead. There's an exciting adventure waiting for you as you step out in faith to serve Him.

Mother Of The New Evangelization

I would like to share one other lesson I have learned about giving a testimony that has helped me tremendously throughout the years. I feel the Holy Spirit has led me to entrust my life and my words of testimony to Mary, Mother of God and Mother of the Church.

Pope Francis tells us in *The Joy of the Gospel, 284*, "She (Mary) is the Mother of the Church which evangelizes, and without her we could never truly understand the spirit of the new evangelization."

The same night I was baptized in the Holy Spirit I opened my Bible at random and my eyes fell upon these words of Mary from Luke 1:46-49:

> *"My soul magnifies the Lord, and my spirit rejoices in God, my Savior, for He has regarded the low estate of His handmaiden. For behold, henceforth all generations will call me blessed; for He who is mighty has done great things for me, and Holy is His name."*

I feel it is significant that the very first Scripture passage the Lord led me to was this beautiful hymn of praise, Mary's Magnificat. Ever since that night I have felt united with Mary in her testimony as I give my own.

No one knows better than Mary how to let "the Word become flesh" in her (John 1:14). No one knows better than Mary how to magnify the Lord (Luke 1:46 55). No one knows better than Mary how to hear the Word of God and keep it (Luke 11:28). And no one knows better than Mary how to accept and carry the whole Church in her heart (John 19:25-27).

What I have done, I urge you to do. Entrust your life and your testimony to Mary. As she did for the people at Cana long ago, she will speak to Jesus about your needs. Aided by her prayers, the water of your simple words will be transformed into the wine of God's own presence. Jesus still performs marvelous deeds when we ask in union with His mother. Be bold as you give your testimony! Bear witness to Jesus! And with Mary I say to you, "Do whatever He tells you" (John 2:5)!

Guidelines For Giving A Personal Testimony

1. Take on the attitude of Christ—one of humility and service.

2. Prepare prayerfully. Seek God for His anointing on you and His blessing on those who will hear you. Seek Him for wisdom about what to say at this time.

3. Organize your thoughts in the form of notes.

4. Respect the time limits imposed on you.

5. Have a beginning, a middle, and an end.

6. Keep it simple. Be natural. Avoid unnecessary details that may distract from the basic Gospel message.

7. Watch your terminology. Be careful not to injure the reputation of another by revealing sins or defects.

8. Submit your testimony to some pastoral leader beforehand for discernment on sensitive issues.

9. Remember the A, B, C's—Audible, Brief, Christ-centered.

10. Be willing to give testimony in person-to-person evangelization. God is not looking for ability so much as availability.

11. Entrust yourself and your testimony to Mary so that she may intercede for you.

12. Be bold. Acknowledge Jesus before men so that He may acknowledge you before His Father in heaven!

Spirit-Filled Evangelizers

In the following pages you will find the personal testimonies of many men and women I am privileged to call friends in the Lord. They are Catholics who have come to an adult commitment to Christ and who are baptized in the Spirit. Most of these testimonies were first given at an event sponsored by the Catholic Charismatic Renewal of New Orleans (CCRNO), the ministry my husband and I have served for over 40 years.

These are stories which have touched me deeply. They were chosen for two reasons. First, they will inspire you as you admire the grace of God at work in lives today. Second, they will illustrate the principles outlined in the first part of this book.

Each testimony is followed by a brief commentary. I have begun with two versions of my own story. The first was given in twenty minutes. The second was given in only three minutes. I want to help you see how the same story can be told with differing degrees of detail.

Come Holy Spirit

A twenty minute testimony given by Patti Mansfield at the 1986 National Charismatic Renewal Leader's Conference in Steubenville, Ohio.

I'd like to begin by sharing with you the very first Scripture passage the Lord ever gave me. A few hours after I was baptized in the Holy Spirit I felt led to open my Bible at random and these were the words my eyes fell on. Every time I have had the opportunity to share what happened at Duquesne, I have begun with these words from Luke, Chapter 1, and they are words found on the lips of Mary, our Mother. "My being proclaims the greatness of the Lord. And my spirit finds joy in God my Savior. For He has looked upon His servant in her lowliness. All generations to come will call me blessed. God who is mighty has done great things for me and holy is His name. And His mercy is from age to age on those who fear Him." Tonight I can say that God who is mighty has done great things for me—not just for me personally, but for all of us. Holy is His name! And His mercy, the mercy that has touched each of our lives so profoundly, is *indeed* from age to age on those who fear Him.

Let me back up a little bit from the day that I received that Scripture passage and tell you something about the events that led up to the Duquesne Weekend. I grew up in New Jersey and was raised in a good Catholic family. I always had a desire to be good and to know more about God, but I felt I didn't know enough about the Catholic faith since I never had the opportunity to attend Catholic school. Many of my close friends were Jewish. When it came time to go to college, I was looking for a good Catholic university where I could study French, a university which had a good ratio of men to women (because I was hoping to marry someday) but especially a place where I could learn more about my faith and meet other Catholic men and women. Through the process of elimination I wound up at Duquesne University, whose full title is Duquesne University of the Holy Spirit. In fact, the motto on the Duquesne emblem is, "It is the Spirit that gives life." Very appropriate!

I started my freshman year at Duquesne taking Theology 101. I found that while it was helpful to take this theology course it wasn't all that I was looking for. The next semester I took another course, then the next year I studied more theology. Slowly it began to dawn on me that what I was really looking for, what I was hungry for, was not just more intellectual knowledge about my faith, not just to **know more about God** but to **know God**—to know Him in a deeper way—to know Him in a more personal way.

I had a good friend who was attending Mass daily. She was part of a Scripture study group on campus called Chi Rho. They would meet once a week to study the Scripture and pray together. This good friend invited me to come to one of the meetings. In fact, she kept after me for a full year to join the Scripture Study. I came up with all kinds of creative reasons why I couldn't go. Basically I was stalling. I felt drawn to know God better but I was also afraid. I was afraid of what He might ask of me. I was afraid that His plans for my life might conflict with my plans for my life, of which I had many. But after about a year I finally met some of the young people in the group. I was impressed by their friendliness and kindness. And so I determined that when I went back to Duquesne as a Junior, I would join them once a week in the Scripture Study. That is what I did.

After a few months we were told that the group would make its yearly retreat. Believe it or not, I had never been on a retreat before in my life. Once again, I had conflicting emotions. I felt drawn to go because I knew it would be an experience of God, and yet at the same time I felt afraid. At first we were told that the theme of the retreat would be the Sermon on the Mount. Fortunately, this was not the theme chosen. Had we studied all the things Jesus said in this discourse, we would have still lacked the power to carry out His commands. The next thing we heard was that the focus of the retreat was going to be the person and work of the Holy Spirit. To prepare for the retreat we were told to read the first four chapters of the Acts of the Apostles and a little book entitled, *The Cross and the Switchblade.*

As I was reading *The Cross and the Switchblade* (for those of you who don't know, it is the story of a Pentecostal pastor, David Wilkerson, who was led by the Holy Spirit to New York City to work with drug addicts), I missed all the references to the Baptism in the Holy Spirit and speaking in tongues. The thing that really struck me was that here was a man living in our own time who could know God's will. God would speak to him in various ways and guide him. I found the desire to be led by the Lord rising in my heart. I kept thinking how wonderful it would be if an ordinary person like me could really know the guidance of God in my life. But I concluded that this kind of guidance must just be for special people like priests, sisters and ministers. Certainly an ordinary student like me couldn't possibly come to know God's will in such a way.

Yet there was enough faith in my heart that when I finished reading that book, alone in my dormitory room, I knelt down next to my bed and said this prayer: "Lord, I believe that I have already received your Holy Spirit in Baptism and Confirmation, but if Your Spirit can be more at work in my life than it has been up to now, then I want it!" And after I prayed the prayer, I opened my eyes and I looked around the room. I don't know what I was expecting to see—a vision, an angel, something spectacular. I didn't see anything, I certainly didn't feel any different and I said to myself, "I will never tell a soul that I prayed this prayer." Believe me, you are not the first people I've told about this prayer! I thought that because I didn't experience anything dramatic in that instant, God hadn't heard my prayer. Do you know what I was praying for? I was praying for the Baptism in the Holy Spirit. I didn't use that terminology, but that's what I wanted.

A few days later, about 25 or 30 students left on retreat. The first night we started with a meditation on Mary. It was presented by one of the professors I knew from theology class. As he spoke about Mary as a woman of prayer and woman of faith, I could see he was a different man. I thought to myself," He seems so calm, so peaceful and happy—almost like he's filled with the Holy Spirit." What I didn't know what that this professor, his wife and two other professors from Duquesne had come into contact with some books about the Baptism of the Spirit. They read *The Cross and the Switchblade* and they read a book called *They Speak with Other Tongues* by John Sherrill. A few weeks before our retreat they attended an interdenominational Spirit-filled prayer group in Pittsburgh. The people there prayed with these four Catholics from Duquesne for the Baptism in the Spirit. We didn't know that, yet I was seeing the evidence of this new release of the Spirit in the peace and the joy of this man as he spoke.

After the meditation on Mary, we had a penance service. In John's Gospel we are told that when the Holy Spirit comes, He will convict the world of sin. And even though this was a very beautiful group of young people, we had plenty of need for repentance. There was a lot of grumbling, complaining, judgments about each other, and factions. As the Holy Spirit came into the penance service that night He was convicting us all of sin. I felt a real spirit of repentance come upon me.

The next day was devoted to the Acts of the Apostles. It was especially significant that the talk on Chapter Two of the Acts was given by a Spirit-filled woman our professors had just met at the prayer group. When I heard she wasn't Catholic, I must admit to you, that I was skeptical. She began by saying, "I really don't know what I'm going to say. I just prayed and asked the Holy Spirit to lead me." This really bothered me. She didn't even have the courtesy to prepare a talk for us! Yet, as this beautiful woman spoke, God was moving. She was so simple. At first I thought she couldn't be for real. She was talking about knowing Jesus Christ as her personal Lord and Savior. She was talking about the power of the Holy Spirit that could be experienced in our daily lives. Although I started out with a resistant attitude, before she finished speaking I wrote in my notes these words: "Jesus, please be real for me. Be real for me the way You are for her."

In the discussion that followed this woman's talk, one of the young men in my discussion group proposed that at the close of the retreat we renew our Confirmation. Each Easter we Catholics renew our Baptismal promises. He proposed that as young adults we invite the Holy Spirit who had already come to us in Confirmation to be released and have His way with us. I had just met the young man who made this proposal, but I agreed that this would be a great idea. I told him that even if no one else wanted to do this, I did. I even tacked up a note on the bulletin board which read, "I want a miracle!" I think it is worth noting that as the Holy Spirit moved later in the evening, He chose to fall upon this young man, David Mangan, and then upon me. We asked for more of the Spirit and therefore we received His anointing.

Saturday night a birthday party was scheduled in honor of some of the students. But the party just never materialized. There was a kind of listlessness. People were just walking around. In fact we had some trouble with the retreat house plumbing. There was no water for a while and we were told they might have to send the whole group home early. But some students were moved to go to the chapel and pray that the water would come back on in Jesus' Name. After praying they turned on the faucet and out came the water full force! Later we heard a plumber had come. How interesting that water is often used as an image to describe the Holy Spirit. Many in the Church today would say, "The water is gone". But in the Name of Jesus there's a fresh flow of the Spirit's living water among us!

Because the birthday party never really started, I decided to go to various parts of the retreat house and gather all the students together in the same room for the celebration. It was at this point that I wandered to the second floor of the retreat house into the chapel. I wasn't going in to pray—just to tell any students there to come down to the party. But as I entered into the presence of Jesus in the Blessed Sacrament and knelt there, I was filled with a sense of awe. I had always believed, by the gift of faith, that Jesus is really present in the Blessed Sacrament, but I had never experienced His glory. As I knelt there, my body literally trembled before His majesty. I felt really scared and I said to myself, "Get out of here quick because something is going to happen to you if you stay in the presence of God." And yet, overriding this fear, was the desire to remain before the Lord.

The young man who was student leader of the retreat came into the chapel and knelt next to me. I described to him what I was experiencing. He said, "Something's going on, something we didn't plan. Just stay here and pray."

As he left me and I knelt there before the Lord, for the first time in my life, I prayed what I would call a prayer of unconditional surrender. I said, "Father, I give my life to You and whatever You want of me, that's what I choose. If it means suffering, then I accept that. Just teach me to follow Your Son Jesus and to learn to love the way He loves."

As I prayed that prayer I was kneeling before the Lord. The next moment I found myself prostrate, flat on my face, stretched out before the tabernacle. No one touched me. In the process my shoes came off my feet. Later I realized that I was indeed upon holy ground. As I lay there I was flooded with a sense of the mercy and the love of God, especially the foolishness of God's love. There's nothing that you and I can ever, ever do to earn or merit God's love. God is a God of love. It's in His very nature to love. We are His people. We belong to Him. God's love just pours out on us no matter what we have done, no matter who we are. The words of St. Augustine so beautifully express what I felt in those moments, "You have made us for Yourself, O Lord, and our hearts are restless until they rest in You." I knew that if I could experience the love and mercy, the tenderness and compassion of God in that way, it was possible for anyone, yes *anyone*, to experience God as well. Although I just wanted to stay and bask in the presence of the Lord, I knew that I needed to share this experience with others. As I rose to my feet I said to the two other students in the chapel, "I pray this will happen to you."

I immediately found the priest who was chaplain and told him all that had happened. He said that the young man who wanted to renew his Confirmation had been in the chapel a few hours before me and he had an almost identical experience. He too was knocked over when the Holy Spirit came upon him. Some people use the expression "being slain in the Spirit." I prefer to say I was swept off my feet by the love of God.

I asked the chaplain with whom I should share this experience. His words have really echoed in my mind for these almost twenty years since. He said, "The Lord will show you. The Lord will show you." Then I asked him how the Lord could use someone as insignificant as me. And he reminded me that when Jesus came into Jerusalem He was seated on a donkey. He can use whomever and whatever He wills!

And as I left this conversation, a few students from the retreat came up to me and said, "What happened to you? Your face looks different!" In second Corinthians St. Paul says that all of us, with unveiled faces, reflecting the glory of the Lord are being transformed from one degree of glory to another. I didn't realize that I looked different, but apparently these girls saw a reflection in my face of what God had done in my heart. I told them I had experienced all that we were talking about that weekend. For a girl who used to be afraid of speaking about Jesus, I suddenly became bold. I took them by the hand and said, "Come into the chapel with me." We knelt before the Lord and I began to pray. This was the first prayer for the Baptism of the Holy Spirit among Catholics. I said simply, "Lord, whatever You just did for me, do it for them! Whatever You just did for me, do it for them!" That was the shortest Life in the Spirit Seminar on record! Alleluia!

Although no one called the party downstairs to a halt, within about half an hour all the students were up in the chapel. God was sovereignly moving. As we knelt there a number of things were happening. Some people were weeping. Later they told us that they felt God's love for them so much they couldn't do anything but weep. Other people got the giggles. They just started laughing and they laughed and laughed and laughed. Some people, like myself, felt a tremendous burning in their hands or going through their arms like fire. Others felt a clicking in their throats or a tingling in their tongues. You have to remember that we didn't know anything about the gifts of the Holy Spirit. We probably could have all spoken in tongues right there, but we did not know how to yield to this gift. One of the professors who had been baptized in the Holy Spirit about a month before, walked in and looked at us. He said, "What's the Bishop going to say when he hears that all these kids have been baptized in the Holy Spirit?" I heard that phrase, "baptized in the Holy Spirit," and I wondered what it could mean. We still didn't fully realize what was happening to us.

Right from the very start, Satan was at work. That night as the Holy Spirit was sovereignly falling and the gifts of the Spirit were being experienced, one young woman said she felt something enter her which filled her with hatred. It was obviously an evil spirit. She felt driven from the place by this spirit and wandered down a road by herself. Someone had to go get her and bring her back. The next day she was in torment. As we were getting ready to leave the retreat house, I spotted her huddled on the ground. One of the professors who was already baptized in the Holy Spirit came and got me. "Come on, Patti, we have to go over and cast out the spirit." I didn't even know if I believed in evil spirits, much less casting them out. But I trusted him. He said, "Command in the name of Jesus that this evil spirit depart." I did as he said and immediately the girl relaxed. She was so relieved, but bewildered. She told us that the night before while everyone was so happy and rejoicing she felt a terrible hatred for what was happening. Then she said that, although she hated everyone in the room,

Spirit-Filled Evangelizers

she hated me most of all. As God's Holy Spirit was sovereignly poured out, Satan immediately sought to harass and destroy the work of God. But the Lord won the victory and He continues to win the victory! Alleluia!

As we returned to Duquesne the words of Psalm 126 describe our experience. "We were like men in a dream. Our mouths were filled with laughter and our lips with shouts of joy. Even the pagans started talking about the marvels God had done. What marvels He did, and how glad we were." I had one classmate say, "What's come over you Patti? If I didn't know you better, I'd say you were drunk!" Of course this delighted me because I had read in Acts 2 that this was the very thing said to the Apostles after Pentecost.

In the weeks that followed we gradually began discovering the gifts of the Holy Spirit—the gift of healing, the gift of prophecy, the gift of tongues and interpretation. Just a few weeks after our experience at Duquesne, we were told that two men who were Cursillo leaders were coming to visit. All I knew about them was that one was named Ralph and the other was named Steve. "Ralph and Steve" were Ralph Martin and Steve Clark! I was keeping a notebook at the time following the retreat and I made the following entry: "Lord, I understand that two Cursillo leaders are coming tomorrow named Ralph and Steve. I know that when You come to them, You'll come to the United States and then to all the world." I didn't even know what their last names were and yet God was revealing to me that He was going to use these two men to spread the Baptism of the Holy Spirit internationally, and He has.

The first Notre Dame conference I attended was in September, 1967. There were fifty of us. We all fit in one small paneled room. Just a few years later, at another Notre Dame Conference, I stood in the football stadium with 35,000 Catholics who had been baptized in the Holy Spirit. Now there are millions of us from all over the world. Only God knows exactly how many people have been blessed with this tremendous experience of the release of the Holy Spirit. It is all God's work! The Charismatic Renewal has spread so widely throughout the Catholic Church in this time because God decided to act in power.

Sometimes I have been asked, because I was at Duquesne, how it feels to have been there at the very beginning and to see what has happened since. My answer is that I feel very united to Mary. I feel very much caught up in the mystery of Mary and of her response to God. The way I would put it to you is this: One "YES" can make a tremendous difference! What one "YES" can do! Mary said "YES" when the Holy Spirit overshadowed her. You know what happened – Jesus Christ was born! And as the Holy Spirit overshadowed us, each of us said "YES" to God and in some way conceived Jesus. Now we have the mission of bringing Him forth to the world. Having been part of this work of the Holy Spirit for twenty years now, I feel I have entered into the mystery of that role of Mary—to embrace the action of the Holy Spirit so that Jesus may be brought forth to the world. It's a very humbling experience. And it is a very awesome experience. For this reason I have made Mary's Magnificat my own: "God who is mighty has done great things for me and holy is His name!"

It is a privilege that the Lord allowed me to be present at Duquesne twenty years ago, but I don't just want to be part of the past and hearken to the things of long ago. I don't just want to be part of the present. I want to be part of the *future* and the tremendous work that God is about! I have felt for a few years now that the Lord is sending a new wave of the Holy Spirit. Those of us who were part of the first wave twenty years ago, we haven't seen anything yet! The new wave has begun but it's still to come. I believe that every one of us is meant to be part of this new wave of the Holy Spirit, this tremendous work of evangelization that's about to break forth. And do you know how we can be a part of it? Just ask God! Just ask Him!

As I sought the Lord for a special word to share with you He led me to read a passage from Luke, Chapter 11. You are probably familiar with it. I'm sure you've heard it many times. Yet as the Lord directed me to this word, it rang true to me in a new way. I felt the Lord say to me, "Patti, ask me for what you need. Ask me for what you need. Have you ever asked me for anything I haven't supplied for you? Have you ever put your trust in Me and found that I let you down? Ask Me for what you need." Jesus speaks to us right now in the words of Luke 11, "Ask and you shall receive. Seek and you shall find. Knock and it shall be opened to you. For whoever asks, receives and whoever seeks, finds and whoever knocks, is admitted. What father among you will give his son a snake if he asks for a fish or hand him a scorpion if he asks for an egg? If you with all your sins know how to give all your children good things, how much more will your heavenly Father give the Holy Spirit (the best of all good gifts) to those who ask Him."

Brothers and sisters, let's believe His word. Let's ask for more and more of His Holy Spirit. As we approach Him we need to have the following attitudes: We are going to ask with humility, because we know we are nothing. We are going to ask with repentance because we are weak, we are sinful, we have made mistakes. We are going to ask with tremendous confidence, not because of who we are but because of who He is and what He has promised us. "Ask! Ask!" He tells us. Let's obey His command.

Mary is with us. She was in the Upper Room at Pentecost. She was with us at Duquesne, and she's joining her prayers to ours right now as we come before the Father. In her Magnificat Mary tells us, "The hungry He fills with good things, but the rich He sends away empty." If we feel our own need for more of the Holy Spirit then we can be sure the Lord wants to fill us! Let's pray, "Come Holy Spirit! Overshadow us in the name of Jesus! We have not seen all of your wonders Lord. We have not seen all of your power. But what we have seen causes us to cry out for more. We want more of

You, Lord, and less of us. We want our lives to be at Your service, at Your disposal, even as Mary's was. Lord, send forth Your Holy Spirit and renew the face of the earth!"

Come Holy Spirit

I gave this testimony in about twenty minutes almost 30 years ago. This is a transcription. Because my personal testimony is tied up with the beginning of the Catholic Charismatic Renewal, I try to blend items of personal as well as historical interest. Starting with a Scripture passage can be effective, especially if it's something that has touched your life in a special way.

Since this testimony was given at a Catholic gathering I felt free to refer to the Blessed Sacrament and Mary. I also wanted to explain the Baptism in the Spirit in terms Catholics could understand; namely as a release of the Holy Spirit—already received in Baptism and Confirmation.

Repeating the prayer I said in the chapel seems to touch people. You too may find that repeating the words you spoke to the Lord in prayer can help people enter into your relationship with Him. Keep it brief.

In this testimony I was asked to emphasize the growth of the Charismatic Renewal after the Duquesne Weekend. Therefore, I didn't use much about my personal life since the Baptism in the Holy Spirit. It's good to find out how the leaders of the meeting want your testimony to fit into the overall program. In this case, my testimony was followed by a time of prayer for empowerment by the Holy Spirit. That's why I ended with an exhortation based on the passage from Luke 11, "Ask and you shall receive."

The Duquesne Weekend

A three minute testimony by Patti Mansfield given at the 1977 Ecumenical Conference in Kansas City.

I feel I can echo the words recorded in Luke 1, "My being proclaims the greatness of the Lord. My spirit rejoices in God my Savior. He who is mighty has done great things for me and holy in His name."

God has always been a part of my life. I knew Him through the love of family and friends, through attending Sunday Mass as a Catholic, through Sunday school instructions, and in His many blessings of health and happiness over the years. But the experience I had in 1967 as a college student at Duquesne University in Pittsburgh brought me into a new dimension of the Christian life that I know now is meant for *all* God's people.

I had a hunger to know God better and this is what led me to choose Duquesne University where I hoped to deepen my understanding of the Christian faith. It was this same hunger for God that led me to join a Scripture study group on campus to learn more about His word. In February, 1967 this Scripture study group made a retreat weekend after reading Acts 1 to 4 and *The Cross and the Switchblade* by David Wilkerson. In preparation for the retreat I prayed in faith that if the Holy Spirit could be more at work in my life than He had been up until then, I wanted it. Through the talks and discussions that weekend I came to see that although Jesus was very important to me I had not yet fully yielded my life to Him as LORD. I was still in control, and because of this His Holy Spirit could not be completely released in me.

On Saturday night of the retreat, we had a birthday party planned for some of the students. During the course of the party I went into the chapel to tell any students still there to come to the birthday celebration. As I entered the chapel I became aware of the presence and the holiness of God in a way I had never known. I began to pray in the depths of my heart a prayer of total surrender. I said, "Father, I give my life to You. Whatever You want for me I want. If this means suffering, I accept it. Only teach me to follow Your Son Jesus and learn to love the way He loves."

In the next few moments I found myself prostrate before God's altar and flooded with a sense of His tremendous personal love for me—a love that seems foolish because it is so lavishly given to us who could never begin to deserve or merit it. In recalling that evening I am reminded of the words of Augustine, "You have made us for Yourself, O Lord, and our hearts are restless until they rest in You." As I rose to my feet I was convinced that what I had just encountered—the love of God our Father, the saving presence of Jesus our Lord, the power of the Holy Spirit—this personal knowledge of God is meant for everyone!

Within an hour the Lord sovereignly called many

of those present at the retreat into the chapel where He revealed Himself and poured out His Spirit upon us. We had planned a birthday party that night. The Lord did too, because that evening marked the birth of the Charismatic Renewal in the Catholic Church.

We returned to campus with a sense of wonder as God opened His Word to us, gave us a new boldness to witness for Him and equipped us with the gifts of the Holy Spirit. Through us, news of the Baptism of the Holy Spirit spread among other Catholics.

These past ten years I have come to know the abundant life that Jesus promises. I have come to know the power of His Spirit working in us that can do *infinitely* more than we can ask or imagine!

One abiding lesson for me has been this: Jesus Christ is Lord! He is all! Our life with Him really *is* the pearl of great price, the treasure hidden in the field worth giving all we are and all we have to possess (cf. Matthew 13:44-46). With each passing year I come to see more clearly that whatever I used to count as gain I now can count as loss. Indeed *nothing* can outweigh the supreme advantage of knowing Christ Jesus my Lord (cf. Philipians 3:7-8). May each of us give our lives to Him anew during this conference that He, Jesus, may be our wealth and treasure, our Lord and our all! Amen!

Spirit-Filled Evangelizers

The Duquesne Weekend

I gave this testimony in 3 minutes! Can you believe it? Because I was only allotted a short time, I had to prepare carefully and speak quickly. I have included this short testimony after a twenty minute version of the same story. I want you to see what had to be sacrificed and yet how much could still be said.

This was given at an ecumenical gathering. Notice the changes in how I refer to Mary and the experience in the chapel. Even though I had only a brief time, I wanted to use many Scripture references since Christians of all denominations share a love for God's word.

The Prodigal Son

A testimony by Rick Tauceda given at a Charismatic Renewal gathering

My mom is here. She's never heard some of the things I'm going to share, but I'm happy she can be part of this meeting tonight. Here goes, Mom.

I was born in Honduras, Central America. My family moved to New Orleans in 1960, and since then I have been an immigrant. I have always felt like an outsider. During the racial strife in the mid-sixties, because I was a dark skinned white, I experienced pressure from both sides. Throughout my life, I felt inferior to other people. I thought I was a nobody and I didn't like myself. I was unhappy and desperately wanted to change.

One day when I was twelve years old, I told my parents I was spending the night with my friend. Instead, we decided to attend an all-night party. The party ended abruptly when the police raided us. My friend and I escaped by breaking a windowpane and climbing through. We ran and ran until we couldn't hear the police sirens any more. I was scared to death. Little did I realize, as my friend and I roamed the streets talking about our near mishap, that I was about to experience the presence of God. In our wanderings we passed a church, and out of the corner of my eye I noticed my

Spirit-Filled Evangelizers

friend making the Sign of the Cross. It bugged me. I wondered why he did that. I thought Christianity was a waste of time. I finally asked him why he made the Sign of the Cross. He told me, "You're supposed to do that every time you pass a church. That's God's house. Jesus is there."

After he said that, I immediately felt God's presence right there on the street. I kept walking and my heart started pounding again. I was shocked to realize that God was there with me. I said, "Lord, forgive me. Forgive me for being bad, for lying, for doing what I did tonight."

That night passed and I soon forgot the Lord. But even though my life was to get worse before I encountered God again, I know that he heard my prayer that night.

In an attempt to escape reality, I started smoking pot, which was a common pastime in high school. By the time I was sixteen, most of my friends had dropped out of school, but I managed to continue, thinking that I would do my parents a favor by getting a diploma. My life seemed empty. I felt thirsty for something, yet I didn't know what. I was going to be a senior in high school, but I didn't have any idea what to do with my life. I thought of becoming a yogi, because I was into yoga at that time. I thought that if I did enough drugs and opened my mind and raised my consciousness I could reach a level where I could communicate with God or something. At that time, I renounced the Catholic faith. I couldn't find anything in it; I couldn't stand to be at Mass. I just couldn't get into it, so I left the church and continued doing more drugs.

I had joined a yoga society and was reading their literature and learning yoga positions. But the more I got into it, the more I felt like I had nothing. The more I meditated and the more I got into being a vegetarian, the more desperate I became. I began to spend more time alone, to withdraw. I would sit in parks or go to the airport by myself and do a lot of thinking.

During this time my best friend's father was attending prayer meetings. He kept telling me about the change Jesus had made in his life. And I did see a change in his life. Every time I looked at him he seemed to have a smile on his face. He would come home from the prayer meetings on Thursday nights and talk to us about Jesus. We would talk back to him about meditation and yoga. He was trying to convert us, and we were trying to convert him. This went on for weeks and weeks.

One Saturday night I was in his kitchen feeling desperate. I knew he had something that I didn't have, but I didn't want to admit it. However, that night I said to him, "Tell me more about your Christianity." He got out his Bible and told me more about the gospel. He quoted one Scripture verse that hit me like lightning. It's the passage in which Jesus said, "I am the way, and the truth and the life; no one comes to the Father but by me." It shocked

Spirit-Filled Evangelizers

me. Here I was, in Eastern religions and drugs, which proclaim, "This is the way, this is the truth and this is the life." And yet, none of them said, "I am the way." I was astounded by the uniqueness of Christianity, and the love of God that was shown through Jesus. In the other religions I was involved in, the whole thrust was to become God-like. In Christianity, God became one of us.

My friend's father went on to ask me a question that he asked at the right place and at the right time. (And I think that is the only time it should be asked—at the right time, in the right place.) He asked me, "Rick, have you ever experienced the release of the Holy Spirit in your life?" I thought I was spiritual, so I said, "Maybe." I didn't want to admit that I hadn't. I said, "Tell me more."

He did and then offered to pray with me that the Holy Spirit would be released in my life. I was desperate so I said okay, not knowing what to expect. So there we were in the living room, and he and his wife prayed for me. As they began praising the Lord, I looked at them, trying to understand what was going on. My friend's father encouraged me to pray to the Lord, and I actually wanted to pray. I closed my eyes, and the moment I said, "Jesus," my resistance completely broke. By the time we were finished, I had prayed in tongues, and I left their house knowing that my life was about to change. And it did.

A few weeks later, I was sitting in front of my house when a friend of mine walked by. I said, "Frank, what are you doing?" When he told me that he was going to a prayer meeting, I knew the Lord wanted me to go. So I went with him. When we walked into the prayer meeting, I saw college kids praising God, and loving one another. Again I knew they had something that I wanted.

I remember one song from the prayer meeting: "For to those who love God, who are called in His plan, everything works out for the good." And I said to the Lord, "God, I love you." That night I committed my life to Him. Immediately I stopped taking drugs, and soon after, I lost all my old friends. I knew that following the Lord was the most important thing in life.

Finally I found that my thirst was being quenched. That emptiness I had known was being filled. In one Scripture passage Jesus tells the Samaritan woman that He is offering living water that will well up inside. When God's Spirit welled up inside me, my thirst was quenched. And when I committed my life to the Lord, I knew that I had found what I had been searching for.

I have been following the Lord for six years, and I am still discovering God's Holy Spirit. I realize how little I know, yet I know how much He has done in my life.

I want to say a word to young people. Since I have come to understand and experience the Gospel, I have begun to realize the meaning of the Church as God's people. Before, I could never relate to the Church, because it didn't make any sense to me.

But now, in a time when people are leaving the Church, I realize how important it is to be part of the Church. I can't abandon what God hasn't abandoned and never will.

Also, the Lord has changed my self-image. I used to compare myself to other people and feel discouraged about myself. I was too skinny, other people had more dynamic personalities, and so on. I now realize that God made me, and He likes me just the way I am. I have also experienced the love and acceptance of God's people. This has revolutionized my life.

I want to close by saying a word to all parents. You know the story of the prodigal son. Maybe you feel as if your son or daughter is far away in a distant land, in the mud. Don't give up on them. They may be on drugs. They may be mixed up. All you have to do is open your arms to them like my mom did. Don't stop loving them. There's *nothing* the King can't do. I've seen dope addicts and homosexuals turn to the Lord. If the King could work in my life, He can work in your children's lives too. The Lord wants you to trust Him, to keep praying and not to lose hope. I thank God that even when I was far away from Him He never stopped loving me and calling me back home.

Rick Tauceda is now living in West Palm Beach, Florida, where he is retired from the Postal Service. He and his wife, Marki, have four children and five grandchildren. Rick now has his own photography business.

The Prodigal Son

Rick's testimony was given in about twenty minutes in the early 80s. I have included it because it's a good example of how effective a young person's story can be. Rick was totally natural and relaxed in his presentation. Everyone was won over when he mentioned his mom at the beginning. A good beginning that endears you to your audience is very important. This was perfect.

Notice that Rick was deeply affected when his friend made the Sign of the Cross in front of a church. His friend also used the name of Jesus and immediately Rick felt God's presence. Using the name of Jesus brings forth His presence in an amazingly powerful way.

The use of the passage from John 14 was excellent because it illustrated the uniqueness of Jesus Christ. "I am the Way, the Truth and the Life." People who heard this testimony, who were not yet believers, were confronted not only by Rick's faith, but by the Word of God itself!

You can see the beautiful humility in this young man as he says he still has so much to learn. Yet he doesn't lack confidence in proclaiming how much God has already done for him.

His closing exhortation to young people and to parents adds strength to his presentation. He is using the special circumstances of his life to the best advantage. Young people will listen to him because they can identify with his struggles. Parents can be encouraged to continue praying for their children. Had he not concluded with this special exhortation his testimony could have remained just an inspiring story with little application to the lives of his listeners. Instead he seized the opportunity to encourage people. "There's nothing the King can't do for you and those you love!"

A New Creation

A testimony by Corinne McCain

"If anyone is in Christ he is a new creation. The old has passed away. Behold the new has come." This passage from Second Corinthians describes exactly what happened to me five and a half years ago when I attended the Life in the Spirit Seminar and received the Baptism in the Holy Spirit.

I knew God even as a little child, yet I always realized that my knowledge of Him was incomplete. I used to think about God as my Father and Jesus as the one who died on the cross for me. All I knew about the Holy Spirit was that I had received the Holy Spirit in Baptism and Confirmation. As I entered my teenage years, I found out that it was the Holy Spirit who guided me and took care of me. Sometimes I would wonder if Jesus could play a greater part in my life. I knew there was more for me spiritually, but I didn't know how to receive it.

As time went on, I got married. I was extremely happy. I loved being a homemaker and a mother. Yet still, even amidst the happiness, I knew there was something about my relationship with the Lord that needed to change. I just didn't know how to make it happen, so I tried to push these thoughts aside.

My husband and I began to prosper. Money became plentiful and we began to experience the luxuries of the world. My husband had an excellent job. He was in line for a big promotion as Vice-President of a very large company. In fact he received the promotion and then our lives began to deteriorate. I saw things happening in my marriage that I didn't like.

Our whole lifestyle had changed. We began to entertain customers. There were a lot of parties, mostly cocktail parties with plenty of drinking. Spiritually, things were going downhill. We would go to Mass on Sunday and forget all about God the rest of the week. When we went to Mass we'd sneak out early so we could get to the tennis court. We joined several country clubs and became active with tennis. In fact, tennis became an important part of my life. After a time, my children even began to miss Sunday Mass.

It's sad to think that sometimes God has to allow suffering to come into our lives to get our attention. This is exactly what happened to me. Within a very short period of time I lost my mother and my father. Between the death of my mother and father, my only sister had a severe heart attack and we almost lost her. I also felt I was losing my children in a way. One got married and the other was in college. The final blow came when, after thirty-three years of marriage, my husband left me. I had to sell my home, which I loved so dearly. After thirty-three years of family life, I suddenly found myself in an apartment, alone. I didn't think I wanted to live anymore. I never will forget the first night that I closed the door and went into my apartment. I had nothing to live for. In fact, things got so bad that I didn't want to go outside, especially if the day was sunny and the birds were singing. I couldn't bear to see a beautiful day because my life was such a shambles.

About this time, someone invited me to make a Life in the Spirit Seminar. I must say that I agreed to go for purely selfish reasons. I thought that if I went through this Life in the Spirit Seminar, all my problems would be solved. I still hoped that my marriage would be healed. I wasn't exactly seeking God for Himself alone but for what He could do for me. But God is so good. He takes us just as we are. That's how I came to Him in the Life in the Spirit Seminar.

I will never forget the night of the Baptism in the Holy Spirit. Everyone seemed to be so filled with the presence of God. Some people wept for joy. But I just sat there, numb. I just didn't feel anything. All the way home that night I kept asking the Lord, "Is this all there is for me?" I went to sleep somewhat disappointed but when I woke up the next morning everything was new. I wish I could put into words everything I experienced. It was beautiful! Welling up inside me was the love of Jesus Christ, my Lord. This Jesus for whom I had been hunting all of my life was really there! I felt Him in a way I had never felt His presence before. I fell to my knees and started crying. Tears were really flowing. The tears of joy I saw others shed the night before were now my tears. Jesus overwhelmed me with His love and mercy! The Holy Spirit had been released in me! I was a new creation!

Suddenly, it was clear what I had been doing all my life. I considered myself a pretty good person. I was a good mother and a good homemaker. Yet I had many idols. It's so easy to have idols. You just don't realize it. I had put my husband, my children, my family, my home, all ahead of Jesus. Jesus wants to be first in our lives. He wants to be our Lord. I had never let Him be first in my heart until then. Once He was first I experienced a joy and a peace that has never left me.

Some things didn't change. I still had all of my family problems, but I slowly learned how to cope. I had Jesus with me now. I knew He was with me to help me in all circumstances. Gradually, I began to get my life together. Jesus helped me through the stages of self-pity and hurt. Yet I didn't always realize how much He was doing for me.

While I was working in a Life in the Spirit Seminar as a discussion leader, someone came in to pray for inner healing. The prayer was being said for those not yet baptized in the Holy Spirit. But God used this prayer to open me up to His grace in a new way. I was the one who was healed! As the prayer was said, I began to realize all the areas in my life that the Lord had touched. I began to see all that the Lord had done for me. But most of all, I realized that God had given me the ability to forgive. I did forgive. Forgiveness was flowing out of my heart for all who had hurt me. And Jesus set me free! He set me free! I know now that the more I submit to Jesus and let Him take over my life, the more He will set me free. If the Son makes you free you are free indeed!

There is a special passage I would like to read. It was given to me during the last session of the Life in the Spirit Seminar by some dear friends and it has meant so much to me ever since. It is from the Book of Revelation, chapter three, Jesus says, "Here I stand knocking at the door. If anyone hears me calling and opens the door, I will enter his house and have supper with him and he with me. And I will give the victor the right to sit with me on my throne as I myself won the victory and took my seat beside my Father on His throne."

What a beautiful promise the Lord is making to all of us! I know now that the door to my heart has to be open every day. It is not enough to open the door just once. I know in my weakness I have a tendency to strike out on my own without Jesus. When I do, I fail. I have to open the door to my heart every day and let Him in. I have to invite Him to be my Lord and Master again and again.

I just want to thank the Lord for waiting for me so long. I want to thank Him for His faithfulness and for His personal love. I only regret that it took me so long to come up to this microphone to give praise and honor and glory to His Holy Name. Praise be to You Lord Jesus Christ! "He gave me beauty for ashes, the oil of joy for mourning, the garment of praise for the spirit of heaviness" (Isaiah 61:3).

Corinne McCain was for many years a pastoral leader in a large prayer group in the New Orleans area. She taught the Life in the Spirit Seminar and had a special ministry to divorced and separated women.

A New Creation

Corinne's testimony took about ten minutes. I have chosen this particular story because it shows such a beautiful simplicity and discretion in sharing about painful circumstances. In a very few words she was able to bring her listener through the events of her life leading up to the Baptism in the Holy Spirit.

She does not criticize nor condemn her husband. Instead, our attention is drawn to the deep work God accomplished in her through the pain of separation and divorce. This kind of a testimony can do tremendous good for people who are suffering the loss of a loved one in various ways.

Once again, the use of a Scripture passage is effective. Corinne was able to appeal to people who have still not made a personal commitment to the Lord as she shares from Revelation about Jesus knocking at the door.

Remember what I said about looking happy and redeemed when you speak? Corinne is radiant and joyful when she speaks about what God has done for her. The passage from Isaiah 61 at the end of her testimony aptly describes the transformation in her life. She is a believable witness.

Notice that Corinne says she regrets how long it took her to have the courage to give a personal testimony. The psalmist says, "I have not hid your saving help within my heart" (Psalm 40:10). And Jesus promises "Everyone who acknowledges me before men, I also will acknowledge before my Father who is in heaven" (Matthew 10:32). Don't hide His saving help and don't hesitate to acknowledge Him before others. His promises of reward are great! Corinne discovered that for herself.

Life Begins At Forty

A testimony by Fr. Harold F. Cohen, SJ

I remember that when I was a youngster, my father used to refer to a book entitled *Life Begins at Forty*. Well, for me, life actually did begin anew at forty. It was on my fortieth birthday that I was giving a retreat for college students from Loyola University in New Orleans. After the night's activities, I slipped away from the students and walked outside by myself. I was dissatisfied with my life as a priest because I felt I wasn't praying as I should. I also knew I was too self-centered. As I walked, I asked the Lord to change me because I knew I couldn't make the necessary changes on my own. I reminded the Lord about His promise in Ephesians 3:20, "His power working in us can do infinitely more than we can ask or imagine."

Some months passed and one day a young man named Jim came from Fordham University in New York to see me. He was being interviewed as a candidate for the Southern Province of the Society of Jesus. I was one of the interviewers. Jim belonged to what was then called a Catholic Pentecostal prayer group at Fordham. I had read about Catholic Pentecostals in 1967 and was intrigued. Even though I desired to go to a prayer meeting someday, I suspected that I would feel somewhat threatened by it. I pictured myself standing on the fringes, observing.

When I first met with Jim, I decided to talk about the Pentecostal movement in the Catholic Church just to break the ice. This was Good Friday, 1969. Afterwards, I conducted the interview for the Jesuits. When we got together again on Easter Monday, I asked more questions about the Baptism in the Holy Spirit. Jim explained that he didn't consider it another sacrament. This relieved me greatly because I was beginning to desire the Baptism in the Holy Spirit for myself. Even though my questions started out of curiosity, before long I found I was seeking God. As I listened to Jim, I quietly asked the Lord in my heart if this experience was meant for me. It seemed to be of God so I said, "Lord, give me the guts to ask."

I finally worked up the courage and asked Jim to pray over me. He was only too glad to do so. He told me to renew the commitment to Christ that I had made when I took my vows as a Jesuit and when I was ordained. I did this, then he prayed for me. Honestly, I was hoping I'd have a great experience of God at that moment. But all I experienced was feeling rather silly having this college student pray over me. I remember that Jim prayed in English, then he prayed in tongues and again in English. Afterward, we took a walk and prayed the rosary together. Nothing extraordinary seemed to have happened, but my whole life changed as a result of that day.

When we parted, I sensed God's presence in a gentle way. But later that night when I went to pray in the chapel, I felt a depth in prayer I hadn't experienced in years. From that time on, my prayer changed considerably. As a priest, this is what I was longing for. I have been much more faithful to seeking God in prayer since receiving the Baptism in the Spirit. This has been a tremendous grace in my life and in my priesthood.

Since 1969 I have seen a number of effects of a new fullness of the Holy Spirit in my life. The main effect is in my ministry. Before the Baptism in the Holy Spirit, I often felt I was trying to minister out of my own strength. I realize that now the Lord is doing more and I am doing less. His power and His gifts are more of a reality in my life. I feel that through my ministry, the Spirit has touched many people to commit their lives to Jesus Christ as Lord. He has used me to help people live out their Christian commitment in an on-going way.

After I received the Baptism in the Spirit, the Lord used me to start two large prayer groups in the New Orleans area. Doors opened for me to bring the Charismatic Renewal to various places in the Southern United States, as well as Mexico, South America, Central America, Hawaii and Australia. I feel privileged to be a part of the great movement of God's Spirit on the face of the earth today.

For the past several years, I have experienced the leading of the Spirit in the area of media evangelization, both on radio and television. I now have programs airing locally and nationally. My desire is to go to all the world on radio and television with the good news of Jesus. Without the anointing of the Holy Spirit I could never minister in this way.

In my own personal life I feel the Lord has been working at continual purification. I have a long way to go, but I look to the future with great confidence and trust. I know God's grace is at work in me and that He will bring to completion what He has begun.

A new life began for me at forty when I reminded the Lord about His promise in Ephesians 3:20. Let me close now with those words: "Glory be to Him whose power (which is the Holy Spirit) working in us can do infinitely more than we can ask or imagine!"

Father Harold Cohen, SJ was a pioneer in the Catholic Charismatic Renewal. From 1969 on, he was used to foster the Renewal throughout the world. He had tremendous gifts as a preacher, teacher and conference speaker. His radio and television ministry, "Closer Walk", was aired in the New Orleans area and on the Eternal Word Network. He died in 2001.

Life Begins At Forty

This testimony took about ten minutes. I have heard Father Cohen give his personal story in much greater detail at other times, incorporating teaching and exhortation. In this brief version he wanted to highlight the changes that took place in his life and ministry as a priest. He is not focusing his testimony on the Charismatic Renewal as a movement or exhorting people to conversion. Instead he is bearing witness to what happened to him.

This kind of testimony is especially effective with other priests, religious sisters or lay people in ministry. It illustrates that with the Holy Spirit, there is always more! Father Cohen is not preaching to his listeners. He's simply telling about the new power he has experienced since being baptized in the Holy Spirit. In certain situations it is appropriate to exhort strongly in a personal testimony. In other circumstances it's better to take a low-key approach. Let the Holy Spirit guide you.

On God's Team Now

*A testimony by Danny Abramowicz,
Former NFL player and coach*

You talk about a Super Bowl! If a Super Bowl football game was one tenth as exciting as serving the Lord, I might think about coming out of retirement! A couple of days ago, I asked the Lord what He wanted me to do in this testimony. I felt as if he said, "Danny, I want you to open yourself inside and let my people see you." So that's what I'm going to do because I want to be obedient.

Until 1967 my life was pretty much like most Roman Catholic boys. I played sports, was an altar boy, attended Catholic grade school, high school and college. In 1967 I was drafted in the seventeenth round (the last round) by the New Orleans Saints. I think they drafted a basketball player right before me. After all, who wants a 5' 11", 180 lb., slow wide receiver? I didn't blame them, but I was still angry. I came to training camp with about a thousand–to–one shot. They were trying to figure out ways to get rid of me. Through the grace of God, I got through training camp.

I remember running down on those specialty teams. They were the guys who would run and hit that wedge. Man, I'd hit those things a couple of times and I came back with blue eyes—one blew north and one blew south! People say, "Danny, you're not very big for a football player." Then I tell them I used to be 6'5"!

About midway through the first year I made it on the specialty team, but I told my wife, "I don't know how long we're going to last in this racket." Then there was an injury to the tight end, and they moved the wide receiver in front of me to tight end. That's when I got my first start in the NFL, halfway through the season. I ended up catching twelve passes for 170 yards and I remained there for the next nine years. It taught me never to get injured.

It might sound like I'm bragging, but I'm not. I'm trying to give you a picture of what my life was like at that point. I am speaking especially to men. I ended up the season catching fifty passes in the remaining seven games and I was the runner-up rookie of the year in the NFL. I said at the end of that season, "Ha! I showed them! I'm going to have a better year next year!" I went into the second year and I had a better year. In the third year I said, "Ha! I'll do better than that!" And I did. I ended up making All-Pro that year and I led the National Football League in receiving. As this was taking place, my popularity grew from a local, to a regional, to a national level. I was into the party scene, the drinking, the discotheque scene. I had it all, man!

This went on through 1974 when I retired from football. You might look at my life in worldly standards and say, "He had it made!" I was All-

Pro, had a beautiful wife, three kids, set a National Football League record—but was I happy and serene? Let's find out.

After I finished with football I said, "Hey! If I did it in football, I'll do it in business!" So I got me a three-piece suit and an attache case and out into the business world I went! I was part of the jet set. We were flying to New York, going here, going there. I got into that three martini lunch scene. Cool! Meanwhile, there's my wife and three kids back home. I know now she had to be praying for me all that time.

My life went on like this for several years. I still remained a Catholic, by the book. You know, go to 11:15 Mass on Sunday and run everyone over trying to get out of the parking lot. My wife was pretty well disgusted with me and I couldn't figure out why. One day she told me, "There's going to be a priest coming to our church to give some talks. Would you mind going with me?" I agreed.

The program at church was going to start on a Monday. I had one of those three-martini lunches and Monday night I came be-bopping into the house and asked if she was ready to go. She said, "I'm not going anywhere with you in that condition!"

That was fine with me. In my arrogance, I put some after-shave lotion on, and off to church I went. The place was packed, so I sat in the back. Before you know it, I pulled one of those doze-off jobs and started to snore!

When it came time for Communion, I had the audacity to jump up and go to Communion. As soon as I got back I said to myself, "Man, I need to get out of here!" So I did. I got outside and then I thought, "You know what I need—I need a drink!" There was a party that night for the present and past Saints football players and their wives. So I went to the party and proceeded to make a fool of myself. I was coming to a turning point.

Over the years I had sometimes felt guilty about my drinking and I'd say to my wife, "I'm gonna stop, hon. I won't do it anymore." Then I would be back drinking again. Sometimes I would vow at nine in the morning that I wouldn't take another drink. But by noon, I was drinking again.

But the morning after that party when I woke up, something was different. I got out of bed and looked at my wife. Then I went into each of my children's rooms and looked at them. I came back to my room and looked in the mirror. It's the first time that I really looked at Danny, and I said, "I don't like this person. If I have to continue on like this, I don't want to continue on. What can I do?"

The only person I could think of was a priest friend. I called him and said, "I need to see you."

"Well, I'm open next…"

I said, "You don't understand, I need to see you right now!"

When I told him I thought I had a drinking problem. He said, "You've come to the right place.

Spirit-Filled Evangelizers

I'm an alcoholic!"

I said, "Man, don't go that strong! I said I just had a drinking problem!"

He sent me to see a friend of his named Buzzy at the F. Edward Herbert Hospital. I didn't even want to admit I was in the hospital for my own problem. It was easier to pretend I was there to visit someone else. I saw Buzzy and he gave me a test of twenty questions to determine if I was an alcoholic. If you miss three questions, you are pretty well an alcoholic. If you miss four, you definitely are. I missed the first thirteen!

He invited me to an Alcoholics Anonymous meeting and I agreed to go without even thinking about it. So on December 15, 1981, a trial, a tribulation in my life turned out to be the greatest thing that ever happened to me. That's the day I attended my first AA meeting. I had the disease of alcoholism. Some of you might say, "Poor Danny!" No, this disease was the greatest thing that ever happened to me because it stopped me. It stopped me from the fast pace we keep in our society. Once I stopped, I started to realize how much I needed.

I went to the AA meeting. It was the hardest thing I ever had to do. I attended several more meetings. I was sober, but I wasn't peaceful or serene. But something was happening. I began to desire to know more about the Lord. I found out about a Bible study class and I said, "No, way!" But I went.

The first time I went in the teacher said, "Open

your Bibles!" Mine had never been cracked so I said, "I just bought this. My other one's worn out." My teacher, Benny Suhor, was a leader in the Catholic Charismatic Renewal. About the third week I was hiding back in the corner and Benny said, "You know, we have a prayer meeting on Wednesday nights over at St. Benilde Church in Metairie. Would you like to go?"

I'll never forget my first charismatic prayer meeting! I walked in and sat down. I thought bumblebees were invading when they prayed in tongues! People had their hands up, waving around. I said, "These people are crazy!" But I couldn't deny the fact that they had smiles on their faces, while I had a frown on mine. I knew I wanted what they had.

Then I was invited to a Life in the Spirit Seminar which introduces people to the Lord and the Baptism in the Holy Spirit. For seven weeks I attended this Life in the Spirit Seminar and it really changed my life. In those seven weeks I came to the realization that for everything to work and be happy for me, Jesus Christ had to be Lord of my Life! I finally gave myself over to the Lord and let Him have control.

You see before that, I was in charge. It was me and booze, my ego and booze. The Lord revolved around me. But it has to be the other way—Jesus in charge and we revolve around Him. I received the Baptism of the Holy Spirit. Once I let the Lord take over in my life, I could stand up and say without a problem, "Hi, I'm Danny. I'm an alcoholic." I didn't

Spirit-Filled Evangelizers

have to worry about what people thought. I just had to worry about having my life right with the Lord. When I made Jesus Christ the center of my life, the Spirit started working in me. Love came inside of me. The anger and resentment had to go. Anger and resentment can't abide in a person who opens up to God's love. Love will win every time.

Now I have a new power to love in my life. The love between my wife and me became stronger and stronger. The love for my family grew stronger. My love for other people became deeper. I couldn't love other people before. I liked some of them, but I couldn't love them with God's love. I feel a greater love for the Church, the sacraments, the prayer group. Because Jesus is now my Lord, love has increased. My priorities have changed. What pronoun did I use earlier? I! I! I! I was always number one. That had to go.

I finally found the peace and serenity I was always looking for. You can't out-give the Lord. The more you give yourself to Him, the more peace and love He gives you. And after all, that inward peace is what we are all searching for. I'm going to tell you something. You'll never find true peace in your life through material things. Ask John Beluschi, Elvis Presley, and Howard Hughes. Ask athletes like me. It's not money and it's not power. It's not any of those things. True peace can only come when each and every one of us establishes a personal relationship with Jesus Christ. Once you do that, other things fall into place.

Maybe some of you are thinking, "I know he's right, but how do I do that? How do I get closer to God?" I'll tell you how. You just ask the Lord in a simple way to show you. Say, "Lord, show me how to make you the Lord of my life." And He'll do it. He might zap you immediately or He might take a long time. With hardheads like me, it took a little longer. But He'll do it because He loves you.

Remember I told you how the Life in the Spirit Seminar changed my life? These Seminars have helped countless people come to know Jesus in a personal way and receive the Baptism in the Holy Spirit. You can make one of these Life in the Spirit Seminars. They are given at Catholic Charismatic prayer groups and renewal centers all over the world. Find out about them. Then come with your heart and mind open and simple like a child and let the Lord touch you.

Jesus is the lifesaver! The lifesaver! Nothing else! Nothing else! The relationship that I personally have right at this moment with Jesus Christ means more to me than anything in the world. I wouldn't give it up for anything in this world! I want to proclaim to you the message that has changed my life. May it change your life too!

JESUS CHRIST IS LORD!

JESUS CHRIST IS LORD!

JESUS CHRIST IS LORD!

Danny Abramowicz is a former NFL athlete and coach who used to reside in the New Orleans area with his wife and three children. He now lives in Chicago. Since his conversion Danny has been active in Alcoholics Anonymous, in working with youth, founding a men's prayer group called "The Monday Night Disciples" and co-hosting a program on EWTN for men called "Crossing the Goal". He is author of Spiritual Workout for Men.

On God's Team Now

This testimony was given at a large conference in New Orleans. In transcribing it, I have tried to preserve the spontaneity, humor and honesty that Danny conveyed. I want you to see how important it is to be yourself and to be natural as you give your testimony.

Danny is a football player. He knows he can reach other men because of that. Here he is speaking "man to man" and it is very effective.

Relating his success in football and in business is not bragging. Instead, it highlights the fact that in the midst of fame and fortune he was still unhappy. Danny's honesty about his alcoholism has encouraged many people to find help for their drinking problems and find the Lord as well.

You notice here as in the other testimonies that there is a very strong proclamation of Jesus Christ as Lord. Danny is very specific in calling people to make the Life in the Spirit Seminar. This is an excellent thing to do. There are often people who want to respond to the Lord after a testimony, but they don't know what practical steps to take.

In a very few words Danny makes clear that the experience of the Baptism in the Holy Spirit has deepened his love for his family, the sacraments and the Church. This is important if you are a Catholic who wants to reach other Catholics.

That Inevitable Question

A Testimony by Courtney Dominique

So, I go the doctor the other day because I broke a bone in my foot and the nurse starts asking me the usual questions: How much do you weigh? How tall are you? Then comes the good ole: Are you single, married, divorced or widowed? And I paused for a moment, wondering how my marital status has any relevance to my foot. Then I find myself not wanting to answer this question with just one word.

I wanted to answer, "Yes, I am divorced, but I am peacefully divorced. My marriage is annulled, and I am doing just fine. In fact, I'm blessed to be where I am today!" But I knew she probably wasn't interested in all of that. My point is—divorce is very complex and so are the range of emotions and ripple effects it creates.

It took some time, some counseling, and a lot of praying to get where I am today. I have been divorced now almost seven years. It's easy for me to remember because my youngest wasn't quite one when my divorce was finalized. As Proverbs 3:5-6 states: "Trust in the Lord with all your heart. On your own intelligence rely not; in all your ways be mindful of Him; and He will make straight your paths."

I had no choice but to trust in the Lord because my life definitely didn't make any sense. I couldn't understand why or how this was happening to me and my poor, precious children. I loved being married. I embraced every aspect of it. I couldn't imagine life any other way. I realized right away that I had to get to work healing myself. I found an amazing Catholic counselor and reluctantly attended "divorce" meetings my parish offered.

I'll never forget the first meeting when the speaker told us not to rush into things because maybe God was calling us to be single Catholics. I almost fell out of my chair!!! As a 30 year old with two children under the age of three, that sounded like a death sentence! Through counseling I was able to understand forgiveness; and the anger that was eating me alive, keeping me up at night, and taking over my life, began to melt away.

As time passed my marriage was annulled, my children were a couple of years older and I was ready to fill the void! I wanted to settle in my new house with someone to share my life with. That's when the anxiety set in. There was this constant nagging feeling sometimes greater than others, but always there. This little part of me was restless and unsatisfied. I was looking and searching for something.

Then one night I was actually able to take a bubble bath (which was miraculous in itself) and I bluntly said to God: "I will give you my heart if you give me peace in return." I instantly felt peaceful, and still do to this day - peaceful with being as the facilitator stated: a single Catholic. Divorce doesn't define me. If someone were to ask, "Who are you?", I certainly wouldn't answer, "A divorced mom with two kids." I would reply, "I am a very blessed child of God with two little souls entrusted to me!"

For obvious reasons, one of my favorite verses is Philippians 4:6-7: "Have no anxiety at all, but in everything, by prayers and petition, with thanksgiving, make your requests known to God. Then the peace of God that surpasses all understanding will guard your hearts and minds in Christ Jesus."

God has always remained the center of my life and it was my faith that sustained me through the dark times. I was also shown God's love through my family and friends who carried me from the very beginning. They still do to this day. As I Thessalonians 5:18 states: "In all circumstances give thanks, for this is the will of God for you in Christ Jesus."

Whatever cross you might bear, big or small, ask for peace and expect to receive it. Jesus' Heart is bursting with mercy and graces for us. He wants to shower us with His unending love if we only ask! Open your heart today to the Holy Spirit and allow a healing to take place.

I now totally embrace my life as it is and can't imagine it any other way. I am, however, open to whatever God has in store for me. God is good... all the time! The next time I go to the doctor, I might just keep a copy of this testimony readily handy for when I get asked that inevitable question!

Courtney Dominique is from Covington, Louisiana, where she is a parishioner of St. Peter Parish. She is mother to two children ages 6 and 8. She is in her seventh year as a Junior High art teacher at Pitcher Junior High. In the past she has been involved in the Divorce ministry. Her sister, Jennifer Blanchard, is the next testimony in this book.

That Inevitable Question

This five minute testimony was extremely effective. Courtney is an attractive, young, single mom. There are many young women in her situation. Courtney's honesty in sharing her story was a source of many graces flowing at our Holy Spirit Women's Retreat in 2014.

It's amazing how much can be said in just five minutes! Remember that the less time you have, the more focused you need to be. This kind of a testimony can be shared on a plane, in a grocery store or at work. Jesus wants to walk with us in every situation and give us His peace. After all, He is the Prince of Peace!

Knock Him Off His Horse

A testimony by Jennifer Blanchard

"For my thoughts are not your thoughts, neither are your ways my ways, says the Lord." (Isaiah 55:8). These words from Isaiah take on a new significance as I reflect on the path that has led me to this stage tonight. It has been long and winding, marked by wrong turns and painful detours. It has not been a path I ever expected to take. Many times along the way I felt hopelessly lost. But God knew just where I was. He allowed me to fall so that He could lift me back up. He allowed me to wander off so that he could bring me home. His ways, indeed, were not my ways. They were infinitely better.

Raised in a strong Catholic family, I inherited my parents' faith. By the time I left home for college, my Catholicism was on "automatic pilot." I was Catholic because I had always been Catholic. I had my faith in my head, but not truly in my heart. I didn't see it as a problem then, that Korey, the handsome man who swept me off my feet, was not a practicing Catholic. He was baptized in the faith, and in the beginning of our relationship, was open to attending Mass. That was good enough for me. Korey and I were married and our two paths became one. We set off on our way, not realizing that we were already lost. We didn't realize how desperately we needed God to lead us or how drastically we needed to change our course.

The warning signs were not far down the road. After the birth of our first son, I realized that I could no longer operate on "automatic pilot," passing along a faith that I wasn't truly living. The responsibility of leading this little soul—and the three others that soon followed—to heaven was overwhelming. What would I teach them? As a mother, I began experiencing a desire to actively embrace my Catholic faith, to truly live what I was teaching my children. I developed a new appreciation for the Church and her teachings. I felt like I was coming home again—the prodigal daughter.

As a father, Korey also felt the same responsibility to his children. The "details" of faith that once seemed only little speed bumps were now massive roadblocks in our path—and in our marriage. In reality, Korey had fundamental disagreements with many Church teachings. He no longer went to Mass and began discussing the search for another faith, one that he would want our children to embrace, as well. Our one path split into two very separate ones heading in opposite directions. I watched my "Catholic" family shatter. The road ahead was dark and uncertain—and all uphill.

I realized, too late, that the faith I had taken for granted mattered more than anything else! In fact, it was really ALL that mattered!!! I began praying for Korey's conversion. Recalling St. Paul's experience, and thinking that my headstrong husband would require something along the same scale, my prayer became "Please, God, knock him off his horse!"

I attended the 2011 Holy Spirit Women's Retreat here and made the Life in the Spirit Seminar during the day on Saturday. I had this prayer on my lips— and I begged God for a miracle. I begged God to bring Korey back to the Church, to touch his heart in an undeniable, powerful way.

When the Life in the Spirit Seminar ended and I was prayed with for the Baptism in the Spirit, I felt like nothing happened. But in the year that followed, everything changed. God did work a miracle in me and in my husband. Only God, in His great providence and love, could have ordained Korey's return to Him. He called Korey through the witness of our eight year old son, in reverent awe of making his First Communion; through the words of a Catholic acquaintance who spent hours defending and explaining the faith to him; through the instant, inexplicable connection to a priest presenting our parish mission; and through powerful experiences in Adoration. I was blessed to witness the unfolding of God's plan for Korey— and, at times, could hardly believe what was happening!!! To give one example of the profound change in our marriage, we were both open to learning about Natural Family Planning. We are now delighted to be expecting our fifth child (another son)!!!

Korey was confirmed in May of 2012, a month after our oldest son received his First Communion. He is now wholeheartedly, joyfully, unbelievably... Catholic. My husband, who was prepared to leave the Church, now attends Mass EVERY morning (rain or shine, at home or on vacation—no matter what!—he now attends daily Mass and spends an hour in Adoration.) Korey has a deep devotion to Mary and the rosary. He is a beautiful witness to our faith and a powerful example to our children—and to me. The man whose faith I prayed to change, I now want to imitate. "Please, God, knock me off my horse, too! Give me the steadfast faith and devotion of my husband!" God is so good!!!

Reflecting on our journey, I am able to see that God used every valley, every wrong turn, every dark night to draw us closer to Him. Although we didn't realize it, there was nowhere in our marriage, nowhere on our journey, that God WASN'T. The same is true for each of you, no matter your mistakes, no matter your suffering, no matter the seemingly impossible situation in which you might find yourself. Have faith! If your life in not unfolding according to your plan, take comfort! It is unfolding according to the plan of our God who sees what you can't see, knows what you don't know, and loves you beyond all measure. "For I know the plans I have for you says the Lord, plans for welfare and not for evil, to give you a future and a hope. Then you will call upon me and come and pray to me, and I will hear you. You will seek me and find me when you seek me with all your heart" (Jeremiah 29:11).

Jennifer Blanchard was born and raised in Covington, Louisiana. She has been married to Korey for twelve years. They are blessed with four children, ages 3-11 and are expecting their fifth. They are members of St. Peter Parish.

Knock Him Off His Horse

During our annual Holy Spirit Women's Retreat, usually the last weekend in January in Lafayette, Louisiana, a lovely young woman came up to me and said she knew someone in my family. She explained that the previous year she had attended our retreat and made the Life in the Spirit Seminar. After receiving prayer for the Baptism in the Spirit, she felt as if nothing had happened. But a year of miracles followed.

Immediately I asked if she would share her personal testimony the next day. She seemed hesitant and declined. Later the family member who knew her told me that it was unlikely such a quiet person would ever agree to speak publicly.

To everyone's surprise and delight, just one year later she agreed to speak and she gave this tremendous testimony. She was amazed when she realized that the day she was speaking "just happened" to be on the Feast of St. Paul who was knocked off his horse. I've often seen her husband Korey and some of their little boys in the Adoration chapel, rapt in prayer, since that time. Yes, Jennifer's prayers were answered, infinitely exceeding all she could ask or think!

Proclaim The Joy Of The Gospel!

God Has Kept Your Tears In His Bottle

A testimony by Judy Hoffmann

Well, children don't come with manuals and when you don't know the Lord, it's a battle raising children. Our son was a challenge to say the least! We changed his schools nine times so the teachers could get off our backs for his cutting seats on the bus, smoking, unscrewing desks, doing drugs, etc. I had a conversion at thirty-four and was forever on my knees. I still have calluses today! I would go in his bedroom in fear that once again he had flown the coop out of the window.

One night my prayer partner had a word that my son was at "the hill". We lived in Houma, Louisiana, at the time and it is flat. But her brother took us out with flashlights to a construction site the kids called "the hill". We saw a place where a little fire was left smoldering with beer bottles and empty Marlboro cigarette cartons. Discouraged, we went home. I was walking in the door at 11 pm and the phone was ringing. My son wanted to tell me that he was alright. I told him I was just walking in from "the hill" since the Lord had told Miss Kay where he was. I heard dead silence on the phone before he hung up. He knew the Lord had his number!

It was a fight with schoolwork from the beginning, and the teachers wanted him on ADD medication.

An administrator at the school told me that there was no hope for my son. When I would drop him off at school in the mornings, he would scream at me and tell me there was no hell and no devil because "I was it" and slam the door. I'd drive away praying in the name of Jesus that Satan would get his hands off of my son. I'd proclaim that my victory was in Jesus. My son told me later that he wore his scapular even in the shower because he knew its promise that the devil couldn't have him.

At 16 he ended up in a coma with spinal meningitis. My prayer partner, Kay, came to meet me at the hospital since the Lord had told her his diagnosis. The doctor was planting in our heads all the bad news of what to expect but I interrupted him. I told him all I wanted to know was what to look for to know that he was out of the woods. He looked surprised at my question but he said that my son would be out of the woods when he would be able to respond when talked to.

Many people were praying; some even kept a prayer vigil all night doing spiritual warfare for my son. The next day the reading was about the healing of Jairus' child. My son spoke that day and was on the road to physical recovery. It didn't shock me because I had confidence that Jesus would spare him.

But when we moved to Lake Charles, Louisiana, my son went from bad to worse. I even asked God why He didn't take him when he was in ICU the year before when his soul wasn't on its way to hell as I perceived it was after our move. One night when he had run away and I was calling my spiritual buddies for prayer, I heard the Lord say, "You haven't thanked Me for this yet." I confessed, "Lord, I'm sorry. I know you love my son more than I do and You know why You are allowing him to do everything he is doing. I trust you". Then I heard the song "I Will Make a Sacrifice of Praise" and my heart understood what it meant to praise him even when my heart was breaking!

At that time I did offer a sacrifice to the Lord of my favorite soft drink. I was a Dr. Pepper addict and I told the Lord that I would never again drink Dr. Pepper if He would show my son that the beautiful gift of sex belongs in a marriage.

Al and Patti Mansfield came to Lake Charles for a conference, and I was graced to go to them for prayer for my son, crying for his soul. Patti told me that she saw the Blessed Mother standing on the side of me catching my tears and presenting them to her Son, Jesus. She gave me the Scripture from Psalm 56:10, "You have kept my tears in your bottle." I was at peace.

The next year at our charismatic conference I bribed my son to go. I knew he needed a new set of "trucks" for his skateboard and $75 sounded good to him, so he came. He had the beginning of his conversion at that conference.

I then sent him to the Holy Land with Fr. Barham and Char Vance. Later she confessed to me that she looked at his long hair, baggy pants and skateboard and figured that his parents had wasted a lot of money sending this kid on a holy trip. She heard God tell her that my son was going to be one of his priests. She hit her ear and told God to repeat that because she knew that she was hearing wrong.

My son eventually joined the Franciscan Friars of the Renewal, Fr. Benedict Groeschel's order. When he made his first vows, promising poverty, chastity and obedience I wept tears thinking about how God had taken my sacrifice of Dr. Pepper to the limit!! He proudly raised his habit to show me his knees and said, "Look, Mom, I have calluses now too!!" God is so faithful. My son was ordained a priest on May 12, 2007. He still uses his skateboard to evangelize the youth of today.

Yes, Mothers, our hope is in Christ Jesus and not one of our tears is wasted!!!!! He holds our tears in his bottle.

Judy Hoffman and her husband Gerald have been married for 41 years. They have 3 biological children and another 2 adopted from foster care.

God Has Kept Your Tears In His Bottle

When Judy first shared this testimony with me, it seemed too good to be true. Then she showed me the ordination day photo. What an answer to prayer! This is a testimony about the power of a mother's prayers. It is also a testimony about God's compassion. God weeps with us when we are suffering because of the lifestyle choices of those we love.

In the following story you will read how Judy's testimony helped strengthen another young mother when her child was sick. We help one another when we bear witness and share our testimonies.

With God All Things Are Possible

A testimony by Stacie Reynolds

Jesus looked at them and said, "With man this is impossible, but with God all things are possible" (Matthew 19:26). I always thought that I understood this verse and its meaning but it wasn't until two years ago that I really got it.

I have a beautiful family. I have a loving husband of seventeen years and five wonderful kids. I am very blessed. I have also been coming to the Holy Spirit Women's Retreat for 15 years. We always speak about planting little seeds as we hear talks and testimonies. I know that over the years the Lord has used this retreat to plant seeds in my heart so that I would be able to deal with all that I would and will encounter in this life on earth.

I was blessed to be raised in a devout Catholic family. My parents and grandparents were active in the Catholic Charismatic Renewal of New Orleans. I was always taught about Jesus and Mary and the love that God has for us. I was able to attend Catholic school for 11 years as well. I got married at the ripe old age of 20 and we had our first child when I was a month shy of 22. Two more kids later the Lord called me to a position in our church parish as a youth minister. Life was good. Youth ministry was my passion and I felt the call to be holy more and more each day. But I had a small issue with control and I would always hold back my complete surrender to the Lord because of fear.

Years passed and I continued on my journey as a youth minister by speaking at large events, and, man, did I love doing this! I would get to spread the Gospel to young people and also get to meet some of the most amazing evangelists from all over. There was one thing that I always felt though, and it was that I didn't really have one of those "moments" that these great speakers would talk about. It also always seemed like those "moments" for them were tragic and really scary or sad, so honestly I didn't want to have a "moment". I actually remember praying to God and telling Him that I wanted to surrender my life to Him and I wanted to pray "not my will but Yours be done," but I was so afraid that He would take something away from me or that something really bad would happen.

In 2008 I attended this retreat and the speaker was Johnnette Benkovic. She was on fire and holy and excited and I thought, "What an awesome example of the kind of person I want to be". She did a talk on Saturday morning on forgiveness and surrender. In that talk she said something that really spoke to me. She said (she was speaking of the loss of her son in a car accident) the bad things that happen in life will happen no matter what…whether we are holy or not, whether we are spiritual or not, those things happen. But when we have God on our side and as the center of our lives, those situations and tragedies will be more bearable.

Two years ago my sweet baby girl, Camille Marie, was diagnosed with cancer. She had AML subtype m5, which is a rare type of leukemia usually found in adults. Camille was 7 months old at the time of diagnosis. We were told at the family meeting that she was very sick and that her chance of survival, if she even made it through the first round of chemo, was less than 10 percent. I remember hearing those words, "Your child has cancer," and everything just stopped. I froze, I couldn't hear anything else, I couldn't speak, I couldn't see anything, except in that emergency room I was not alone. Of course there were other people there - my husband, the doctor, the nurse, but it wasn't their presence I felt. It was the presence of our holy Mother Mary and of Jesus, each with a hand on my baby, crying right along with me.

Camille's journey was a rough one. There were lots of needle sticks and surgeries. Six intense treatments of chemotherapy were given to her over a seven month period. She was hospitalized for six months in New Orleans, all while my other four children were home in Covington with my husband. It was trying on my family. I felt pulled in different directions. I wanted to always be at the hospital with her but I also wanted to be at home with my other kids. Here is a "retreat seed". Miss Patti had told me years ago, it isn't the quantity of time you are with your children, but the quality of the time spent with them. I made darn sure that I had quality time with all of my kids at that crazy period.

It was hard on Camille and as a mom that was so hard for me. I would cry almost every night and ask the Lord to take this suffering from her and give it to me. I would beg this all the time. I had to figure out some suffering I could offer for my daughter in order to help ease hers. There was nothing, or so I thought. Then I remembered at a past women's retreat a lady shared what she did when her son was going through a really tough time. She gave up Dr. Pepper as a sacrifice to help get her son through his trial. She said how much she loved Dr. Pepper and so do I! I gave up all soft drinks during Camille's treatment as a sacrifice for my baby. This was another "retreat seed!"

I drew a lot of strength from Mary our Mother and felt a huge connection to her because she had to watch her child suffer just as I did. I even felt during the times of treatment, when I had to watch my baby suffer so much, that Mary was holding me as I held Camille. I drew much comfort from this. My relationship with Our Lady is strong because I learned so much about her from Fr. Harold Cohen, who had such an extraordinary relationship with our Mother…another "retreat seed!"

I am proud to say that my baby girl is three years old and has been completely cancer-free for over two years. Praise God!

"It is impossible for man, but with God all things are possible". I always thought that meant God could do anything and make anything happen. That is true, He can, but for me it means something different.

WITH God all things are possible. Because of the life I have and the upbringing I have had and these retreats I have attended and the people I have encountered, all of these things blessed and placed by God in my life, I am able to withstand ANY and ALL things that come my way.

Stacie Reynolds and her husband Lonnie live in Covington, Louisiana, and are the proud parents of five children. She continues to be active in youth ministry with the Catholic Charismatic Renewal of New Orleans.

With God All Things Are Possible

This testimony was given several years ago and Camille is still cancer-free, thank God! Stacie's grandparents and parents were baptized in the Spirit and passed on their faith to her. Her testimony shows that it's not enough to come from a devout family. Each person must make a commitment to follow Jesus. To Stacie's credit, she availed herself of the opportunities for spiritual growth around her and has become a strong and valiant woman.

You can see how much the testimonies of Johnnette Benkovic and Judy Hoffman influenced Stacie and helped her when she was met with the cross in her own life. We really are members of one another and can share each other's lives at a deep level in the Spirit.

Stacie does a beautiful job of showing the power of Our Lady in this testimony. Mary's presence is real, active and loving. Reaching out for her help in the sorrows of life helps us to bond with her.

Proclaim The Joy Of The Gospel!

The Woman I Was Created To Be

A testimony by Yvette Fouchi

Thirty years ago, I married a handsome, irresistible man. We lived a continuous stream of fun adventures. We even helped to prepare other couples for marriage through Pre-Cana and Evenings for the Engaged.

Our first child was our son, Frank Dana, who was born alive three months premature. My amazing, tiny little boy had captivating, big dark eyes and dark wavy hair. After one, valiant day of life, he died in my arms. I was numb and thoroughly confused. How could God have let this happen? Not long after we had Frank Dana, I got pregnant twice more. Our babies, Kellen Michael and Christina Marie, each died in first trimester miscarriages.

The fourth time I got pregnant, I had surgery at 14 weeks, lots of medical intervention, months of bed rest and much prayer. Our healthy miracle baby, Chantel Liana, was born only three weeks early. She was absolutely the most beautiful baby I still have ever seen. She is now an extraordinary, holy 24 year old woman, with a strong heart for serving God.

Our perfect marriage turned out to be not so perfect. Ten years after saying the "forever I do," we divorced. Overnight I went from a confident, secure stay-at-home mom to a terrified single mother who was determined to provide the most stable home environment possible. I did all I could to let my daughter know she was loved and treasured. I was her room mother, Girl Scout leader, and team mom.

Especially right after the divorce, Chantel and I had some really rough moments. We missed the family life we had previously enjoyed, but together we forged a new way of living. I got through those days one day at a time, sometimes just part of a day at a time. I felt overwhelmed. The nights I had cried myself to sleep before the divorce turned into sleepless, restless nights after the divorce, trying to sort out what I could do to regain some sense of control. It took me years to get that I didn't have control over anything. I did have major issues, including childhood sexual abuse. I was in need of lots of healing, but I didn't know that. I begged God, with my whole being, to help me in whatever way He wanted.

My spiritual transformation skyrocketed when I watched my mother die of lung cancer 10 years ago. She was downright jubilant about meeting Jesus, her very best friend. I wanted that joy and peace.

As I started to pay more attention at Sunday Mass, God planted a seed in my war-torn heart that made me want more of Him. I found myself soaking in graces everywhere. I started going to daily Mass and returned to the Sacrament of Confession. Through prayer, especially after receiving the Eucharist, and in Adoration, I discovered that

I was deeply, personally loved—by Jesus, Love Himself. A new chapter in my life and mission was beginning.

It was not easy or pretty and it certainly wasn't overnight. But, in His infinite mercy and compassion, God gently led me out of confusion and despair, towards a life lived abundantly, becoming more each day the woman I was created to be. Now, as I walk up the aisle to receive Jesus in the Eucharist, He calls me by my new name—His Beloved. He invites me to enter into an intimate, forever covenant relationship with Him that is based on sacrificial love. My "Amen" is my YES. I am hopelessly in love.

Seven years ago, during a CCRNO Women's Day of Refreshment, Patti said at the last minute of the day, "This wasn't on the schedule, but I feel that the Lord wants us to pray over the women here." Quickly, we all lined up. I prayed for direction. I had felt God preparing me for something, but I didn't know what. During that prayer, a clear image came to me with the words "Save My Babies" and I could see myself teaching. Pro-life work hadn't been on my radar, but that day led to the beginning of my pro-life ministry. I now sidewalk counsel in front of abortion mills. I have also been invited to give pro-life workshops and talks at Notre Dame Seminary, universities, high schools, youth groups, churches, state conferences and on the radio.

Perhaps the Lord may be calling some of you here this weekend to begin to engage more actively

Spirit-Filled Evangelizers

in pro-life work. It would be so awesome if more people would give a public, loving witness, by just praying the rosary in front of an abortion mill in your area. I have been told by many women and men that on the morning of a scheduled abortion, they had prayed for a sign from God. If someone was out on the sidewalk praying, they would just drive right past the abortion mill and figure God would somehow be there to see them through. The people on the sidewalk were not even aware that their presence had made a difference at all. I have had the privilege of experiencing the difference they made—in meeting some of those beautiful babies as a result of someone just being out there. Sadly, I have also spoken with many post-abortive men and women, who had prayed the same prayer, but no one was there.

The Lord called me to a whole new ministry. If you ask this weekend, He might have something special and completely new just for you!

Talking about special, this summer, remaining as a lay person, I will become a consecrated celibate, recognized by the Church as living eternally with Jesus as my Bridegroom. In living out my profession, I will permanently strive toward focusing my entire life more intensely towards God through the evangelical counsels of poverty, chastity and obedience, in the secular condition.

God is faithful, offering unexpected new beginnings each and every day, for me—and for you. Don't be afraid to say your own "yes" to God and His will in your life. Be prepared to let Him sweep you off your feet and into His arms! Amen!

Yvette Fouchi has four children: three already with the Lord and one here on earth named Chantel. She has worked as a med tech for over 30 years. Yvette has entered consecrated life as a consecrated secular with the Franciscans in a secular institute called the Missionaries of the Kingship of Christ. She is actively involved in pro-life work.

The Woman I Was Created To Be

Yvette shares about some common heartaches suffered by women, yet she does so with great tact. No one is accused or exposed in this testimony. The focus is entirely on the person of Jesus and His love.

Since her conversion Yvette has become a strong pro-life warrior with many babies who have been saved through her ministry. In this testimony one can see how deep the transformation can be in a person's life. She also gives witness to the beauty of a consecrated single life in the world. She is a radiant witness.

The first time she shared this story, her daughter, Chantel, was present and led everyone in an entrustment to Our Lady. Mother and daughter were quite an inspiration. In less than ideal circumstances Yvette shows that it is possible to raise children to know, love and serve the Lord.

You Have The Heart Of A Twenty Year Old

A testimony by Odelia Champion

I live in Mercedes, Texas, just five miles from the border between Texas and Mexico. I am 78 years and have been a widow for 17 years, so please bear with me, because I am not a public speaker. My reason for being here is to give glory to God for all the wonderful things He has done in my life—especially in my "golden years." Praise God!

Fourteen years ago, I started doing missionary work in Canales, Mexico with Sister Eveline whom I loved dearly. She was the first missionary to go there. Sister Maureen joined us later. The children from Canales called the sisters *"madres"* which means "nuns". They call me *Monjita* (little nun).

People in Canales are very poor. Most of their homes have dirt floors, no electricity or running water. But they do have a lot of faith and I will say, they are survivors. We would go there once a week. We take them beans and rice and whatever else we can. Their vegetable gardens consist of cactus which is what they eat most of the time. They need clothes but it is hard for us to get them across the border because it is illegal. However, we manage to bring some clothes by wearing three and four shirts and putting some under the car seat. Last week I wore seven sweaters! I hope we don't have anyone here who works on the border!

In June 1998, Sister Eveline was forced to retire because of illness and return to St. Francis Convent in Tiffin, Ohio. I went through a very difficult time, thinking I was too old to continue my ministry, but I promised Sister Eveline that I would. Cindy, my daughter, knew what I was going through, trying to decide if I was too old to continue my ministry of serving the poor in Canales.

In 1999, Cindy brought me to the Holy Spirit Women's Retreat sponsored every January by the Catholic Charismatic Renewal of New Orleans. While I was on retreat, I attended the last part of a Life in the Spirit Seminar. As a young lady placed her hands on me to pray, I had a wonderful but unusual experience. I had barely started to tell her my situation and my concerns, when I started crying and mumbling some sounds that I could not control.

After I finally stopped, she told me not to be afraid and that I had just been speaking in tongues. She then said, "You have the heart of a 20 year old and you are going to be surprised at the things you are going to do in the future." It was then that I decided to continue my ministry.

In May 1999, I instructed 13 children who made their First Communion. I am not a teacher but I taught them, trusting God to use me because there was no one else to do it.

In February, 2000, Sister Eveline took a turn for the worse. I was told she had only a few months to live. Right about that time, in my parish church, the priest announced that someone was donating a new Blessed Mother statue. We had statues of Our Blessed Mother and the Sacred Heart of Jesus.

I asked Father if we could have the old one for the people of Canales and he agreed. I was very excited and I said to myself, "Well, we have the Blessed Mother. Where are we going to put her?" Right away I answered my own question: "In a church!" Right then and there, I decided to build a church to be dedicated to her in Canales.

For several weeks, I was in constant prayer. I asked the Lord to guide me. I told Him that if He wanted me to do it, I would do all that was in my power, but that He had to open doors for me.

Having worked in a bank for many years, I talked to them about getting a loan. Even though they never make unsecured loans to anyone over 65 years old, they agreed! To this day, God has led me all the way. I spoke to several groups of retired teachers and asked they if they would help me raise funds and they said they would!

With their help plus the help of many more people, we started construction in June, 2000. Within six months, the church has been built! It is called *"Nuestra Senora de la Merced*, Our Lady of Mercy." Here are some pictures which I have to show you. We still have some work to do and many bills to pay, yet we had the consecration of the church on the 31st. Praise God! Sister Eveline passed away in August but I felt her presence and could almost hear her saying, "Good job!"

We plan to use the church building for multiple uses such as to celebrate Mass, have classes for Communion, Confirmation, and so on, and even use it as a shelter during bad weather.

We have been very busy, to say the least. And I am not finished yet. Since people have to go 10-15 miles to get medications, I am looking at some land next to the church to build a small clinic and have retired nurses go there once a week. In the meantime, we take aspirins, cough medicine, and some other medications for the people when we go each week. With God all things are possible.

So my message to you is this: please, no matter how young or old you are, get involved in some good projects to help people. For the young, there is so much for you to do. Try to visit nursing homes. The people there love to see young faces. Some of my friends think they are too old. I tell them, if you have a car, give those who don't have one a ride to church, to the grocery store or the doctor. Those who do not have a car, call a friend or neighbor just to talk. Invite them for coffee or see what kind of help you can render. Everyone can do something to reach out to others.

As for me, I thank God every day for the gift of life and for allowing me to serve Him. The more I give of myself, the more blessings I receive, and you will too. My mother died when I was six. The Blessed Mother has been my refuge and my friend. I close by saying, "Come Holy Spirit, fill the hearts of the faithful and kindle in them the fire of your love."

Spirit-Filled Evangelizers

Odelia Champion lives in the Houston area. She continues to be an inspiration to all who know her.

You Have The Heart Of A Twenty Year Old

In December of the Jubilee Year 2000, I was a speaker at a Magnificat Luncheon for Women in Houston, Texas. One of the organizers named Cindy drove me to the airport. In the car were her attorney husband and her mother, Odelia. I had noticed Odelia at the luncheon since she is an elegant looking lady who had served as a hostess. She seemed like a sweet person and, just to make conversation, I asked Odelia to share her testimony with me. As we drove along, I heard this magnificent story you have just read.

I could scarcely believe this testimony: a 78-year-old woman built a church for the poor in six months time! Her son–in–law told me that from a legal point of view, the whole thing was miraculous. Usually just obtaining the necessary permission takes much longer than six months. I had no idea on that ride back to the airport, that I would meet a modern day apostle to the poor.

On the third weekend of January each year, the Catholic Charismatic Renewal of New Orleans sponsors a Holy Spirit Women's Retreat now held in Lafayette, Louisiana. We gather over 500 women from the entire Gulf South for the weekend. It was at our retreat in 1999 that Odelia was baptized in the Spirit and received her word from the Lord that she had the heart of a twenty year old and that she should do what He has put in her heart. Therefore, I felt it would be important for her to share her personal testimony with our women.

I asked her for a five-minute testimony. "Just tell them the same story you told me," I begged her. Odelia was very frightened at the prospect of standing up in front of 500 women and speaking. But I persuaded her to write out her testimony and I also promised to help her sort through it. When she presented me with this wonderful testimony, I had very few suggestions for improvement.

On Sunday morning of the retreat when Odelia stood up to speak, her legs were trembling so badly that her clothing was moving from side to side. We arranged for her daughter, Cindy, to stand on one side of her and for her granddaughter to stand on the other side for support. In spite of her nervousness, this was one of the most effective five-minute testimonies I have ever heard! What she lacked in confidence as a public speaker made no difference. The Lord had more than supplied her with love, sincerity and zeal.

When Odelia finished speaking, the women on retreat streamed to the stage to speak to her. There must have been over 50 women who wanted the chance to tell her how much she had helped them and many of them made a financial contribution to her ministry. Without asking for a penny, Odelia inspired these women to want to do their part in reaching out to the poor.

When I met Odelia's daughter in Houston in 2014, she told me that her mom had indeed built a clinic for the poor in Canales and a school as well! What power there is in the baptism in the Spirit! It really is a New Pentecost for a New Evangelization!

I included her story here to inspire any retired people who may be reading this book. Many Christians are being called to a "second career" in the Lord's service after they retire. There are many "Annas and Simeons" out there who need to open up to the new work the Lord is calling them to. Ask the Holy Spirit to come upon you as He came into Odelia's heart. Then you too will be surprised at your new work. No one is too young and no one is too old to serve the Lord and bear witness to Jesus.

Proclaim The Joy Of The Gospel!

Lord, It's All In Your Hands

A testimony by Carlos Munoz, Jr.

In March, 2001, I received my monthly newsletter from Our Lady's Youth Center in El Paso, Texas, a ministry my husband and I help support financially. This testimony was sent by my friend, Fr. Rick Thomas, a Spirit-filled Jesuit priest who was a pioneer in the Catholic Charismatic Renewal. Much of Fr. Rick's work was with the poor in El Paso, Texas and Juarez, Mexico. Fr. Rick wrote, "From time to time the Lord has multiplied food in our efforts to feed needy brothers and sisters. The first time was Christmas, 1972. The latest incident was in late 2000." Then Fr. Rick published the story of Carlos Munoz, Jr., a volunteer at the Food Bank. Here is the amazing testimony in Carlos' own words:

That day we had been in Juarez, Mexico, shopping in the market. I only bought one box of oranges. As we were driving up to the Food Bank, I saw all these people, all these moms and children, eagerly gathered around to receive food. I felt really bad because I knew deep inside that there wasn't going to be enough oranges to take care of all these people. I felt really sad and began to pray really hard to the Lord.

I pleaded, "Lord God Almighty, You know what is needed here. I know that there are not enough oranges to go around to all these children and all these mothers, but if it be Your will, Lord, You can supply the need for all these people."

We went ahead and started to distribute the fruit. I had one box of oranges and Juanita Patterson had one box of bananas. I just kept praying to God, "Lord, it's all in Your hands." When I started, my mind was prudently thinking, "Just give everybody one orange." But then all of a sudden there was something telling me in my heart, "Give them two!" I decided to listen to what was in my heart rather that what was in my mind.

The children were in one line and the moms were in another. I wasn't really looking inside the box because I was afraid to. I just concentrated on each beautiful face in line and told myself, "I'll just give out the oranges until the box goes empty."

I gave each person two oranges and never looked into the box. I focused on each person—their eyes, their smiles—while handling out the oranges by twos. I finished distributing to the children in line and then turned to the moms in line. Before I knew it, Juanita, who had been handling out bananas beside me, was no longer there. She had run out of bananas in her box. I just kept handing out oranges. The lines got smaller and smaller, and all the children around had two oranges a piece and so did all the mothers. There was nobody left.

I finally looked down into the box and couldn't believe my eyes. The box was still ¾ full! I was stunned. My heart felt very warm. I felt the presence of the Lord there. Warm tears streamed down my face.

God Almighty is so awesome! There is a God out there. He loves us abundantly. If you have faith in Him and pray in your heart, really pray to Him, if it is His will, He is going to supply. He is going to give you what you need. He is going to take care of His people, like He did that day. I felt so much love, so much peace. Only our Lord Almighty could multiply the food!

Carlos Munoz, Jr. has served in Our Lady's Youth Center as a volunteer. His faith is an inspiration and a challenge to the rest of us!

Lord, It's All In Your Hands

Since I received this testimony in the mail I have used it wherever I have traveled around the world with great effect. What a proclamation of the living Lord Jesus! Carlos is saying through this story: HE'S ALIVE! Jesus Christ is the same, yesterday, today and forever! (cf. Hebrews 13:8). Everything He did that we read about in the gospels is still happening and not just in a figurative way. HE'S ALIVE! Each time a personal testimony is given, it should contain this astounding truth: JESUS IS ALIVE. He's still intervening in people's lives and changing them.

This is not a testimony about conversion or healing or Baptism in the Spirit. It is a testimony about a particular intervention of the Lord in Carlos' life and ministry. Such a story can do much to build faith in other people. It built my faith tremendously.

When I first read Carlos' testimony in March, 2001, I was not in need of oranges. However, at this time we were in need of funds to hire a youth minister. My husband and I were tempted to feel discouraged and we didn't know where to begin to find the funds for this position.

But after reading about the multiplication of the oranges, faith in Jesus began to rise in our hearts. We imitated Carlos' prayer of faith and turned the situation over to the Lord. "Lord, it's all in your hands." This was Carlos' act of faith. His faith begot faith in us. And the more we put confidence in God's provision to His children, the more we freed His hand to work. In fact, within a few months, the Lord provided for our need for funds to hire a youth minister. Praise His Name!

Carlos is so simple and straightforward in his testimony. He's not a highly educated man. He doesn't use fancy words. He just tells his story. He is a credible witness to the glory of God. God used Carlos' testimony and He will use yours as well.

I believe that as Pope Saint John Paul II exhorted the church of the new millennium to "put out into the deep and lower our nets for a catch," (cf. Luke 5:4), we will see more miracles like this one. It may not be in the multiplication of fish or oranges (or it may...with God ALL THINGS are possible), but it may be in creative new ways to evangelize, to use the media, to capture the hearts of our youth, to meet the needs of our elderly. Be open to exercise your faith through prayer on behalf of those in need and watch what the Lord will do!

Your Personal Pentecost

To prepare for Vatican II, Pope Saint John XXIII called the whole Church to pray this prayer: "Renew Your wonders in this our day as by a New Pentecost." I remember praying that prayer as a child, never dreaming that I myself would experience that New Pentecost through the Charismatic Renewal.

You have read many testimonies of people who have been baptized in the Spirit and you've heard about a course called The Life in the Spirit Seminar. The Life in the Spirit Seminar is simply a tool that was developed by Ralph Martin at the beginning of the Charismatic Renewal to present the basic gospel message. The seven teachings of this Seminar are designed to help Catholics make or renew their commitment to Jesus Christ as Lord and Savior and to pray for the Baptism in the Spirit. For millions of Catholics the world over, it has been the vehicle to release the graces of the sacraments of Baptism and Confirmation.

If you have not been baptized in the Spirit, I strongly urge you to seek this grace. It's possible to have your Personal Pentecost too. If there is not a Life in the Spirit Seminar available in your area, I have good news for you!

Dr. Ralph Martin and Renewal Ministries has recently produced the entire Life in the Spirit Seminar as a DVD set. It is aptly entitled *As By A New Pentecost* and the teachers in this Seminar are all leaders in the New Evangelization.

The DVD set may be used over a seven week period, on a weekend retreat or in a one day format. You may take part in this Seminar in the privacy of your own home, in your parish church or small group. People all over the country are coming into a new life in the Spirit by means of this Life in the Spirit on DVD. There is even a session in which David Mangan and I lead prayer for the release of the Spirit and the gift of praying in tongues.

This Life in the Spirit DVD, *As By A New Pentecost*, is available at www.renewalministries.net. I highly recommend it!

On the Renewal Ministries website you will also be able to access prayers and other resources to help you enter more deeply into a life in the Spirit.

Come Holy Spirit!

I would like to close with the words of our wonderful Holy Father, Pope Francis. Here he expresses his longing for a new coming of the Holy Spirit:

> *"How I long to find the right words to stir up enthusiasm for a new chapter of evangelization full of fervor, joy, generosity, courage, boundless love and attraction! Yet I realize that no words of encouragement will be enough unless the fire of the Holy Spirit burns in our hearts. A Spirit-filled evangelization is one guided by the Holy Spirit, for he is he soul of the Church called to proclaim the Gospel....I implore him to come and renew the Church, to stir and impel her to go forth boldly to evangelize all peoples" (The Joy of the Gospel, 261).*

Other Resources by Patti Mansfield

Magnificat: A Mother's Reflections on Mary

As By A New Pentecost: The Dramatic Beginning of the Catholic Charismatic Renewal

Teaching CDs including:

The Duquesne Weekend: My Personal Testimony
Holiness
More Than Conquerors: Lessons in Spiritual Warfare
Seeking the Face of Jesus
Consecration to Mary
Be Mary
The Gift of Tongues Explained
Women Encounter the Love of Jesus
Come Holy Spirit!
Do You Want to Be Baptized in the Spirit?
Yielding to the Charismatic Gifts

To order these resources, please contact the Author:

Patti Gallagher Mansfield
Catholic Charasmatic Renewal of New Orleans
P.O. Box 7515
Metairie, LA 70010-7515
Tel: 504-828-1368
email: info@ccrno.org
www.ccrno.org